THE FRESH FRUIT COOKBOOK

THE FRESH FRUIT COOKBOOK

New Ways
with Traditional Favourites

PAM CARY

The Crowood Press

First published in 1988 by
The Crowood Press
Ramsbury, Marlborough,
Wiltshire SN8 2HE

British Library Cataloguing in Publication Data

Cary, Pam
  The fresh fruit cookbook: new ways with traditional favourites.
  1. Cookery (Fruit)
  I. Title
  641.6'4   TX811
  ISBN 1 85223 093 2

Dedication

For Renee and Peter — I love you very much

Acknowledgements

Many thanks to Toshiba for the loan of the Toshiba Delta Wave microwave
oven in which many of the recipes were tested.

Typeset by Grassroots, London N3
Printed in Great Britain by
Billing and Sons Ltd, Worcester

Contents

Introduction

Having been born in sunny California, I spent the early years of my life where juicy oranges and other exotic fruits grew outside the back door just waiting to be picked. However, it was only moving to Britain that made me realise, and come truly to love and appreciate, the enormous variety and selection of fruit which is available throughout every season.

A whole new world opened up to me as I began to write this book. Through research I explored fruits from centuries past, and discovered the important roles they played in establishing a much envied heritage. I discovered cultivated and wild varieties which, unfortunately for most of us, never reach the more accessible shops and supermarkets, and therefore remain much of a mystery. It is always worth while investigating where such fruits can be obtained, and perhaps, too, it is worth taking an outing into the countryside, to experience the wild and home-grown varieties at their best. Fruit you pick yourself, from along footpaths, country lanes, or at official pick-your-own farms, always seems to taste so much better than the shop-bought variety. Better still, try growing your own!

Throughout this book, I have left it very much up to you to pick the varieties of fruit you like best, or those which are available at the time. It is important always to use good quality, ripe fruit for the best results with any dish. Most fruits, excluding the citrus varieties, continue to ripen once they are picked. So, if you find the fruit you buy is not quite at its ripest and best, leave it for a few days at room temperature — it's well worth the wait.

I have also included here some freezing and microwave tips so that you can use seasonal varieties all year round. I hope you enjoy this book as much as I enjoyed writing it.

Notes on Ingredients and Equipment

The finished fruit dishes will depend on three important factors: correct weighing, the correct method of preparation and the best of wholesome ingredients.

Flours

1   100 per cent wholemeal: this is the whole grain ground to a coarse or fine flour meal. Wholemeal is high in fibre and very nutritious. Many of the recipes in this book can be made with wholemeal flour (unless otherwise stated). Wholemeal flour tends to absorb more water than ordinary white flour so this should be borne in mind.

2   Soft plain flour: this is lower in gluten than other flours and is therefore suitable for cakes, short pastry, biscuits and puddings. A little cornflour added will improve the texture of flour confectionery. Baking powder should be used in conjunction with plain flour to aid the texture where necessary.

3   Self-raising flour: this is ideal for many pastry and bread recipes.

4   Baking powder: this aerates scones, cakes, sponges and pastry by producing carbon dioxide which expands the dough structure to give lightness in the final product.

Sugars

1   Refined white caster and granulated: these are the most commonly used sugars in baking, although they should be used in moderation.

2   Raw sugar: this is unrefined and contains sugar's natural minerals. It can be used in fruit cakes and breads, as well as sweets and confectionery.

3   Demerara sugar: this is more refined and can be used for decoration purposes.

4   Muscovado sugar: a range of partially refined or unrefined sugars used in many baked goods.

5   Dark brown sugar: this contains a certain amount of moisture as well as minerals and is ideal for dark fruit cakes, fudges and candies.

6   Molasses: a dark syrup used mainly in ginger or other spicy goods.

Fats and Shortenings

The fats used in baking produce the necessary richness, shortness, volume and colour, and improve the keeping qualities of the finished article.

1   Butter: a dairy product, whose flavour remains right through to the finished dish. Ideal for pastries of all kinds and many other dishes.
2   Animal fats: if you are concerned about the use of these then replace them with fats low in polyunsaturates — choose from vegetable margarine, olive, corn, nut and sunflower oils.
3   Fresh dairy cream: single, double and whipping cream are all used in cooking to fill and decorate many varieties of baked goods, gateaux and desserts. These can also be used to thicken and enrich sauces.

Eggs

Both yolks and whites are used in many recipes to enrich, aerate, stabilise and colour breads, cakes, sponges, sweets, meringues, soufflés, desserts and sauces.

Nuts and Seeds

Full of protein, high in vitamin B and minerals, products containing nuts are extremely healthy and delicious. Try them in cakes, salads, desserts — almost anything. There are many to choose from, including almonds, hazelnuts, walnuts, peanuts, cashews, coconuts and brazils.

Seeds have become popular ingredients in all forms of cooking — like nuts, they are protein-packed. The list is endless but try sesame, poppy, caraway, pumpkin and sunflower. They can be used to decorate everything from salads to desserts.

Flavours, Seasonings and Spices

Flavours are occasionally added to improve the overall taste of a dish. However, use only natural essences such as vanilla, lemon, orange, almond, etc. For a more exciting impact, try adding liqueurs to desserts and cream dishes.

Of the seasonings, salt should be used sparingly at all times. Sea salt is the best available, but it is often more convenient to use table salt.

Pepper should always be freshly ground for best results.

There is now a huge variety of spices available and they invite experimentation, so be adventurous and try a few of the less well-known ones. You'll be pleasantly surprised!

CHOOSING FRUIT

There are many different types of fruit used in the recipes in this book. A few basic points to remember are:

1   Always choose the freshest fruit you can find as this will make a great difference to the outcome of the recipe.
2   Fruit which is in season is infinitely more appealing than frozen fruit, so shop around and find out what is available.
3   Don't choose fruit which is bruised or damaged in any way. Select only healthy, well-formed fruit; that which appears ripe or almost ripe is the safest bet for success in the kitchen.
4   Always wash fruit thoroughly before using it, and remove any stalks or leaves which may still be attached.
5   When storing fruit for a few days in the refrigerator, make sure delicate fruit does not get squashed or damaged. It is always best to use fruit as soon as possible after buying, as this will mean the final dish is as near perfection as it can be.
6   The best fruit of all is that which you have grown yourself, so give some thought to planning your fruit garden — in future years you will have a ready supply of top quality produce with which to impress your family and friends.

EQUIPMENT

A small, but good quality, range of equipment will take a great deal of the hard work out of every cooking assignment.

1   Electric equipment: an electric mixer, food processor or blender will be of enormous value for mixing up ingredients, producing purées, and for the many other routine jobs involved in cooking.
2   Mixing bowls: these are always useful so try to build up a collection

of bowls of different sizes.

3 Rolling pin: wooden, china or plastic will be sufficient, but make sure it is clean before use.

4 Whisk: a balloon shape is best for whisking cream and meringues.

5 Spatulas: these are very useful for all manner of jobs.

6 Sieve: a good wire sieve will be invaluable for straining juices and purées.

7 Pastry brush: used for glazing and basting, bristle or nylon types are both suitable.

8 Other useful items: sharp knives, pastry cutters, piping bags and tubes, measuring jugs, baking sheets, baking tins (often springform tins are the best), greaseproof and kitchen paper, double and single saucepans, cling-film, foil, a cheese grater and skewers.

Ovens

A good reliable oven is essential. Microwave ovens are increasingly popular, but although they reduce baking times by many minutes, in some cases they do not produce a particularly strong colouring (on breads for example). Therefore, you might consider finishing in a conventional oven for best appearance results.

FREEZING

By following these easy freezing instructions you can successfully preserve many seasonal fruits to enjoy all year round.

Apples

The best time to buy home-grown apples, ideal for freezing and at bargain prices, is between September and November. For freezing in slices, choose those which are firm and of the best quality. Peel, core, slice or chop, and steep in 700ml/1¼ pints water and the juice of 1 lemon for 15 minutes. Dry on kitchen paper and open freeze on trays lined with greaseproof paper until frozen solid. Seal in boxes or bags. Storage: 1 year.

Soft fruit is best puréed before freezing. Make sure you remove any blemished parts first. Storage: 6 months.

Blueberries

If you plan to store the blueberries for just a short time, they may be frozen on open trays and then stored in plastic bags. Otherwise, first blanch the fruit for 30 seconds to 1 minute to keep the skins tender, then cool and pack. Alternatively, crush the fruit and pack with sugar. Storage: 1 year.

Cherries

All cherries can be frozen, but the red, black and morello varieties are the best. First stone the fruit to preserve the flavour. For long-term freezing it is best to freeze in sugar syrup with lemon juice to prevent discoloration, adjusting the sugar content according to the sweetness of the cherries. For storing, use very firm containers as the juice tends to remain liquid. Storage: 1 year.

Red and Black Currants

Currants may be frozen raw, cooked or pulped. If freezing raw, choose only top-quality, ripe fruit. Freeze dry or sugar-packed, or in sugar syrup. Storage: 1 year.

If freezing as pulp, storage: 8 months.

Currant juice may also be frozen in ice-cube trays, then stored wrapped. Storage: 6 months.

To freeze fruit for making jam, the currants should first be blanched for 1 minute. Storage 1 year.

Gooseberries

If freezing gooseberries whole, it is best to choose fruit that is still hard and slightly underripe. Gooseberries may be dry or sugar-packed, or they may be frozen in sugar syrup. You do not have to top and tail before freezing as you will find this much easier when the fruit is frozen. Gooseberries also freeze very well stewed and sweetened, or cooked, sweetened and then sieved. This is excellent to keep for making fools and sauces. Storage: 6 months.

Peaches and Nectarines

It is best to freeze peaches and nectarines in sugar syrup or sugar-packed. First stone the fruit and slice. Poach in a little water with sugar or honey, to taste, and with a little fresh lemon juice to prevent discoloration. Freeze with the syrup. Storage: 6—8 months.

Pears

Raw pears tend to lose flavour, colour and texture when frozen unless each piece is first dipped in lemon juice and then covered with a sugar syrup. For best results, peel, core and halve the pears, poach in honey or sugar water and freeze with the syrup. Storage: 8 months.

Plums

All plums freeze very well, but it is best to use top quality fruit when it is just ripe. First stone the fruit to prevent the flavour from changing. Freeze in sugar syrup with added lemon juice for best results. Alternatively, cook, sweeten and purée. To make sure the plums do not lose their colour when first exposed to the air from frozen, open them just before serving or cook straight from frozen. Storage: 1 year.

Rhubarb

Rhubarb is ideal for freezing and can be stored in a variety of ways. You can simply wash, trim the ends, drain well and pack and freeze. Storage: 3 months.

To keep rhubarb longer, however, and to preserve the colour and taste, it is best to blanch the fruit first in boiling water for 1 minute, chopped or whole. Rhubarb may also be stored as pulp or in sugar syrup allowing 275g/10oz sugar for every 575ml/1 pint liquid. Storage: 1 year.

Raspberries

Freeze only top quality fruit which is ready to eat. First discard any fruit that is blemished or shows signs of deteriorating and freeze on trays, dry-packed or sugar-packed. Eat slightly chilled from the freezer or cook from frozen. Storage: 1 year.

Soft, overripe fruit is best sieved, sweetened and stored as pulp. Storage: 8 months.

Strawberries

For freezing strawberries whole, use only top quality, fresh and ready-to-eat fruit. Unfortunately, strawberries tend to turn very mushy when thawed, so it is best to eat them when they are still slightly chilled. Softer fruits are best poached and sweetened, or pulped with a little sugar and lemon juice. Freeze in firm containers. Strawberries are especially suited to dry and sugar packing and storing in sugar syrup. Dry, large strawberries are best sliced and frozen in syrup. Storage: 1 year.

FRUIT AND THE MICROWAVE

Several recipes in this book include alternative cooking methods using a microwave. Microwave ovens preserve the full flavour and fresh colour of fruit, so they can be an ideal way to cook many nutritious and attractive fruit puddings, desserts, savoury dishes, and even preserves. Here are some basic handy hints for making the most of your microwave, including a useful chart for using them in cooking fruit.

All microwave instructions in this book are given for a 650 watt output oven with 9 power levels, 9 being high power. Those with different microwaves should take this into account when calculating the correct timings, but remember, it is better to undercook than to overcook. Dishes can always be put back into the oven for a few seconds more if necessary.

Notes

1   Because microwaves preserve the natural sweetness of fresh fruits in season, fruit desserts normally need less sweetening than when cooked the conventional way.
2   Always arrange the fruit evenly in the dish for best results.
3   Fruit may be poached in a little unsweetened fruit juice instead of water and can then be used for making fools and mousses.

4   Poach fruits until soft, then blend to a purée and serve as a sauce with a whole range of dishes.

5   Frozen fruits may be cooked straight from frozen on high power, but stir frequently. The high proportion of natural sugar causes very fast cooking, so watch carefully.

6   Frozen fruits that will be used for cold puddings and desserts need only be partially defrosted in the microwave. Allow them to stand to complete the defrosting process and to prevent the fruit from becoming too soft and collapsing.

7   Soft fruits, such as peaches and raspberries, need not be covered when defrosting.

8   Use your microwave for easy peeling of citrus fruits. Heat on high power for about 30 seconds. You will also find that this heating produces more juice and is an ideal way to make marmalade. To peel soft fruits such as peaches, pierce the skin before heating. Cook on high power for about 25 seconds.

9   Always cook fruit on high power and allow for standing time to complete cooking.

BLANCHING

Blanching fruit is very similar to cooking. It simply means plunging the fruit into boiling water for a few seconds in order to soften them. Always pick fruit which is in good condition. Careful preparation will affect the blanching time.

Microwave Fruit Cooking Guide

Fruit	Quantity	Preparation	Cooking Time (Minutes)	Standing Time (Minutes)
Apples	450g/1lb	Peel, core, slice and add 75g/3oz sugar; cover	6—7	3
Apricots	450g/1lb	Halve, stone, sprinkle with sugar to taste and very little water; cover	6—8	3
Black and Red Currants and Blackberries	450g/1lb	Trim, immerse in water and add sugar to taste; cover	5—8	5
Cherries	450g/1lb	Wash, add very little water and sugar to taste; cover	4—5	3
Gooseberries	450g/1lb	Halve, stone and add sugar to taste; cover	4—6	3
Pears	450g/1lb	Peel, core, quarter and add very little water, sugar to taste and 1 pinch cinnamon; cover	7—9	5
Plums	450g/1lb	Wash, stone, halve, sprinkle with sugar to taste; cover	4—6	5
Rhubarb	450g/1lb	Trim and cut into 2.5cm/1in pieces, add very little water, sugar to taste and grated rind of 1 lemon; cover	9—10	5
Raspberries and Strawberries	450g/1lb	Wash, hull, add sugar to taste; cover	3—5	5

CHAPTER 1

THE APPLE AND PEAR ORCHARD

'There is no kind of fruit better known in England than the apple or more generally cultivated. It is of that use that I hold it almost impossible for the English to live without it, whether it be employed for that excellent drink we call cyder, or for the many dainties which are made of it in the kitchen.'

So wrote Richard Bradley in his *New Improvements of Planting and Gardening* in 1718. For centuries the British have been considered experts regarding the cultivation, varieties, quality and cooking of this ancient fruit. Today, with more than 80 varieties to choose from for baking, frying, stewing, pies, sauces, jams, chutneys, drinking and just plain, sweet eating, the British apple reigns supreme. The best known are Cox's Orange Pippin, Newton Wonder, Laxton Superb, Granny Smith and Golden Delicious for eating raw and in salads. For cooking, stewing and puréeing, choose Grenadier, Lord Derby or Bramley's Seedling. For cooking pies and tarts it is best to choose an apple which has plenty of flavour, but one which will also keep its shape, such as Cox's Orange Pippin or Newton Wonder. Whatever variety you choose, however, look for firm, well-coloured and unblemished fruit.

Perhaps the pear is considered today more as a dessert fruit, but as far back as the seventeenth century specific varieties found their way into the great kitchens of Europe, and in the past, as still today with a little imagination, symbolised the romance of England.

'Her cheek so rare a white was on;
Who sees them is undone;
For streaks of red were mingled there,
Such as are on a Catherine pear,
The side that's next the sun.'
Sir John Suckling,
'A Ballad Upon a Wedding', 1641

Everyone has their particular favourite pears for cooking and eating, so try these recipes with those you like best. But be adventurous too, and try those lesser known varieties that find their way to the fruit market stall. They will open up a whole aspect of England's heritage.

Apple and Ham Fritters

Serves 6   Preparation time: 35 minutes   Cooking time: 12 minutes

Fritters with a difference! These delicious little surprises are best served immediately and are super as an appetiser, breakfast or brunch treat.

550g/1 ¼lb cooking apples, peeled,
  cored and sliced
1 tablespoon sherry
225g/½lb ham, cut into small pieces
50g/2oz candied lemon rind
1 teaspoon lemon rind, finely
  grated
2 egg whites
125ml/4fl oz apple cider
125ml/4fl oz whipping cream
2 tablespoons unsalted butter,
  melted and cooled
1 tablespoon lemon juice
125g/5oz plain flour
50g/2oz sugar
2 teaspoons baking powder
1 teaspoon bicarbonate of soda
½ teaspoon salt
¼ teaspoon each cinnamon and
  nutmeg
Oil for deep frying
Sugar to sprinkle

Pre-heat the oven to 140°C/275°F/Gas Mark 1.

---

1   In a bowl mix together the apples and sherry and place to one side for 15 minutes.

---

2   Mix the ham, candied and fresh lemon rind and add to the apples. Whisk the egg whites until thick. Add the cider, cream, butter and lemon juice and beat together. Sift the flour with the sugar, baking powder, bicarbonate of soda and salt. Sift once more with the cinnamon and nutmeg and add to the apple mixture, combining well. Leave to rest for 10 minutes.

---

3 Line a baking tray with kitchen paper. In a heavy-based saucepan heat the oil to 190°C/375°F. Drop tablespoons of the fritter mixture into the hot oil and cook until golden brown (about 2 minutes each side). When cooked, place on the lined baking tray and keep warm in the oven as frying continues. Serve hot.

Serving suggestion: Serve with a sprinkling of caster sugar.

Liver with Apple and Mustard Sauce

Serves 6   Preparation time: 10 minutes   Cooking time: 25 minutes

225g/8oz unsalted butter
3 red apples, cored and quartered
  (unpeeled)
12 slices calf's liver
Salt and freshly ground black
  pepper
125ml/4fl oz sherry
225ml/8fl oz whipping cream
125ml/4fl oz beef stock
6 tablespoons herb mustard
Watercress to garnish

---

1   Melt half the butter in a frying pan and sauté the apple slices until lightly browned. Remove and keep warm. Wipe out the pan with kitchen paper.

---

2   Sprinkle the liver with salt and pepper. In the frying pan melt the remaining butter and cook the liver according to taste. Remove and keep warm. Pour off any remaining fats in the pan and put the sherry into the pan. Boil until reduced to a glaze-like consistency. Add the cream and stock and boil gently until the mixture coats the back of a spoon. Remove from the heat and beat in the mustard.

---

3   Adjust the seasoning to taste. Spoon some of the sauce on to individual plates and top with the liver. Spoon over the remaining sauce and garnish with apples and watercress before serving immediately.

Serving suggestion: Serve immediately with a crisp salad.

Trout with Apples and Almonds

Serves 4   Preparation time: 5 minutes   Cooking time: 15 minutes

A slight variation on the traditional Trout Almandine.

4 trout, cleaned, with head and tail
  left on
40g/1½oz plain flour
½ teaspoon salt
Freshly ground black pepper
50ml/2fl oz milk
100g/4oz butter or margarine
50g/2oz almonds, sliced
2 apples, peeled, cored and thinly
  sliced

1   Rinse the fish under cold running water and pat dry with kitchen paper. On a large piece of greaseproof paper combine the flour, salt and pepper. Dip the trout in the milk, shake off any excess and roll in the flour mixture until completely covered.

2   In a large frying pan heat 50g/2oz butter until golden. Add the trout and sauté on each side for about 5 minutes until browned. Be careful not to break the fish. When cooked, remove the fish to a warmed serving plate. Add the remaining 50g/2oz butter to the frying pan and, when melted, add the almonds and apple slices. Sauté until browned. Pour the almonds, apples and butter over the fish and serve immediately.

Serving suggestion: Serve with plenty of fresh vegetables and boiled baby potatoes.

Fruit-stuffed Poussins

Serves 6   Preparation time: 15 minutes   Cooking time: 1 hour

The stuffing for these small, succulent birds is full of flavour and makes them a festive dish or a lovely centre for any dinner party. Poussins are well worth searching out for their unique taste.

6 poussins
2 oranges
225g/8oz unsalted butter
½ onion, peeled and chopped
2 cooking apples, cored and
* chopped (unpeeled)*
100g/4oz seedless green grapes
2 tablespoons parsley, freshly
* chopped*

25g/1oz fresh breadcrumbs
½ teaspoon dried thyme
Salt and freshly ground black
* pepper*
6 rashers bacon, cut in half
225ml/8fl oz sherry
Fresh watercress to garnish

Pre-heat the oven to 180°C/350°F/Gas Mark 4.

1   Rinse the poussins under cold water and pat with kitchen paper. Grate the orange rind and reserve. Cut each orange in half and use to moisten the inside and outside of the poussins, gently squeezing the juice from each piece.

2   In a frying pan melt half the butter and cook the onion over a low heat until soft. In a bowl mix together the apple, grapes, parsley, breadcrumbs, orange rind and half the thyme. Pour over the butter and onion mixture and combine well. Stuff each poussin with the mixture and place the stuffed bird in a roasting pan. Season and add the remaining thyme. Place 2 half bacon rashers on each bird and dot with the remaining butter. Pour the sherry over and cook for 1 hour, basting frequently.

3   When cooked, make a gravy with the juices by reducing to about two-thirds over a moderate heat.

Serving suggestion: Serve the poussins garnished with watercress and with the gravy served separately.

Apple Toffee Pie

Serve 6—8   Preparation time: 15 minutes   Cooking time: 3 hours

I discovered this lovely combination of flavours when making a banoffi pie (bananas and toffee) and only had apples in the larder. The crisp apples, sweet, creamy toffee, and coffee-flavoured cream are something to dream about.

For the filling:
400g/14oz tin sweetened condensed
  milk
4—5 dessert apples, cored, peeled
  and sliced
275ml/½ pint whipping cream
½ teaspoon instant coffee

For the biscuit crust:
250g/9oz plain digestive biscuits,
  crushed
100g/4oz butter or margarine,
  melted

1   To make the toffee, place the whole tin of condensed milk (unopened and unpierced) in a saucepan of boiling water and boil for 3 hours. Keep an eye on the water level and do not allow it to boil dry. Remove the can, cool slightly and then place in the refrigerator until thoroughly chilled.

2   To make the biscuit crust, combine the crushed biscuits with the melted butter until well mixed. Spoon into a 23cm/9in pie dish and, using the back of a metal spoon, press down well into the sides and base of the dish. Chill thoroughly in the refrigerator.

3   Open the tin of condensed milk and you will see that it has turned to a thick, brown toffee. Spread this over the biscuit base. Cover the top with the apple slices. Whip the cream until thick. Dissolve the coffee in a very little water, add to the cream and mix in well. Spread the cream over the apple and chill slightly before serving.

Serving suggestion: Serve in thin wedges because this pie is deliciously rich.

Apple and Blackberry Crunch

Serves 4—6   Preparation time: 10 minutes   Cooking time: 40 minutes

Apples and blackberries were simply made to go together. Here is a different version of the very popular crumble, made with oatmeal.

For the filling:
450g/1lb cooking apples, cored,
  peeled and sliced
225g/8oz blackberries, trimmed
100g/4oz sugar
1 tablespoon flour

For the oatmeal crumble:
100g/4oz butter
50g/2oz sugar
50g/2oz soft brown sugar
50g/2oz plain flour
50g/2oz oatmeal
1 teaspoon ground cinnamon
Butter to dot

Pre-heat the oven to 180°C/350°F/Gas Mark 4.
Microwave: cook on high power for 8—10 minutes; allow to stand for 5 minutes before serving.

1 In a bowl mix together the sliced apples, blackberries, sugar and flour.

2 To make the crumble, combine the butter, sugars, flour, oatmeal and cinnamon in a bowl and rub together until the mixture resembles breadcrumbs.

3 In a baking dish put half the apple mixture and top with half the crumble. Repeat the layers using all the remaining mixtures, and dot the top with butter. Bake for 40 minutes until well browned. Serve hot or cold.

Serving suggestion: This crumble is best served hot with cream, custard or vanilla ice-cream.

Baked Apples
with Vanilla Sauce

Serves 4   Preparation time: 20 minutes   Cooking time: 40 minutes

For the apples:
4 medium cooking apples
150g/5oz brown sugar
100g/4oz raisins
50g/2oz walnuts, chopped
1 tablespoon grated lemon rind
1 tablespoon cinnamon
3 tablespoons cider
2 tablespoons unsalted butter

For the sauce:
15g/½oz cornflour
275ml/½ pint milk
1 tablespoon unsalted butter
1 tablespoon sugar
1 teaspoon vanilla essence

Pre-heat the oven to 190°C/375°F/Gas Mark 5.
Microwave: prepare the stuffing for the apples as described below and fill each apple. Place in a shallow, round dish and pour the cider into the base of the dish. Cover and cook on high power for 6—6½ minutes, depending on the type of apple. Serve with the sauce.

1   Remove the apple cores without cutting through to the bottom. Using a sharp knife, cut a shallow indentation around the middle of the apples and reserve.

2   In a bowl mix together the brown sugar, raisins, walnuts, lemon rind and cinnamon. Fill each apple with this mixture to within 5mm/¼in of the top. Pour a little cider over the stuffing of each and dot with butter. Place in a baking dish and bake for 40 minutes until tender.

3   Meanwhile make the sauce. Mix the cornflour to a paste with a little of the milk. Pour the remaining milk into a saucepan and heat but do not boil. Pour on to the paste and mix well. Then return to the pan. Cook, stirring, until the sauce thickens and simmer for 2 minutes. Remove from the heat and add the butter, sugar and vanilla. Mix together thoroughly. Serve the warm sauce over the baked apples.

Serving suggestion: These apples may be served hot or cold.

Lil's Apple Cake

Serves 8—10   Preparation time: 30 minutes   Cooking time: 1 hour

My Aunt Lilian is always in demand for her luxurious 'no fail' apple cake!

For the filling:
1.1kg/3lb cooking apples
50g/2oz sugar
125ml/4fl oz water
2 slices lemon

For the pastry:
450g/1lb self-raising flour, sifted
300g/11oz sugar
175g/6oz butter
2 egg yolks

Pre-heat the oven to 180°C/350°F/Gas Mark 4.

---

1   Peel, core and slice the apples and place in a saucepan with the sugar, water and lemon slices. Cook over a gentle heat until the apples are just soft. Drain the juice, remove the lemon and allow to cool.

---

2   To make the pastry, rub together the flour, sugar and 100g/4oz butter until the mixture resembles fine breadcrumbs. Add the egg yolks and mix together well. Line the bottom of a 23cm/9in springform tin with half of the pastry mixture, pressing down well with the back of a spoon. Fill with the apple mixture and sprinkle with the remaining pastry. Dot the top with the remaining butter and bake for 1 hour. Release the tin from around the cake and gently transfer to a serving dish.

Serving suggestion: Serve hot or cold with whipped cream or vanilla ice-cream.

Variation: For a slightly spicier version of this cake you may like to add 1 teaspoon of cinnamon and 100g/4oz raisins to the apple mixture. Continue as directed.

Chicken Fruit Salad

Serves 4   Preparation time: 10 minutes

For the salad:
3 red apples
2 firm pears
Juice of 1 lemon
1 head of chicory
175g/6oz young celery, chopped
50g/2oz flaked almonds
50g/2oz raisins
350g/12oz chicken, cooked
1 crisp lettuce, shredded

For the dressing:
150ml/¼ pint natural yoghurt
4 tablespoons mayonnaise
*Salt and freshly ground black
    pepper*

1   Chop 2 of the apples, reserving the third for the garnish. Chop the pears without peeling them. Sprinkle with the lemon juice to prevent discoloration. Cut the chicory into rings.

2   In a large bowl mix together the chopped fruit, chicory, celery, almonds and raisins. Chop the chicken meat into even-sized pieces and mix into the salad.

3   For the dressing combine the yoghurt with the mayonnaise and season to taste. Mix thoroughly into the salad.

Serving suggestion: To serve, line one large or 4 individual serving dishes with a bed of shredded lettuce and top with the salad. Slice the reserved apple, sprinkle with a little lemon juice and use to garnish the salad.

Mange-tout Shrimp

Serves 4—6   Preparation time: 15 minutes   Cooking time: 30 minutes

This dish can be served as a main course (for 4 people) or as a delicious starter (for 6 people).

450g/11b mange-tout, trimmed
6 tablespoons unsalted butter
3 Bramley apples, peeled and
  thickly sliced
2 tablespoons sugar
1 small onion, finely chopped
700g/2lb uncooked shelled
  shrimp
125ml/4fl oz white wine
175g/6oz tarragon mustard
(or any mustard)
175ml/6fl oz double cream

1   Boil the mange-tout in a saucepan of salted water until just tender (approximately 2 minutes). Drain immediately and place in the refrigerator to chill.

2   Melt 2 tablespoons butter in a large frying pan and sauté the apple slices until just tender. Do not allow them to go mushy. Sprinkle over the sugar, bring up the heat and sauté until brown and caramelised. Remove the apples and set aside.

3   Melt the remaining butter in the same frying pan and add the onion. Cook until transparent and then add the shrimp. Increase the heat and sauté until cooked. Remove the shrimp.

4   Pour the wine into the frying pan and over a high heat reduce the liquid by two-thirds. Stir in the mustard and beat well. Add the cream and simmer uncovered for 10 minutes. Add the chilled mange-tout, apples and shrimp to the cream sauce and simmer for 1 minute. Serve immediately.

Serving suggestion: Serve with individual portions of rice.

Apple Coleslaw Salad

Serves 6—8   Preparation time: 10 minutes

This is a very refreshing, crunchy salad which makes a wonderful addition to any barbecue, picnic or summer luncheon.

600g/1½lb red apples, cored and
  thinly sliced (unpeeled)
250g/9oz cabbage, shredded
225ml/8fl oz soured cream
3 tablespoons lemon juice
1 tablespoon sugar
Salt and freshly ground black
  pepper
2 tablespoons poppy seeds (optional)

1   In a large bowl toss together the sliced apples, cabbage, cream, lemon juice, sugar, and season to taste. Cover and chill in the refrigerator.

2   Just before serving, toss thoroughly and adjust the seasoning as necessary. Sprinkle with poppy seeds if preferred.

Serving suggestion: Serve in one large bowl or on individual plates.

Pear Custard Flan

Serves 6—8   Preparation time: 40 minutes   Cooking time: 35 minutes

For the pastry:
190g/7½oz plain flour
150g/5oz butter
50g/2oz sugar
2 egg yolks

For the custard:
65g/2½oz sugar
2 eggs
50g/2oz plain flour
425ml/¾ pint milk
1 teaspoon grated lemon rind

For the topping:
3—4 firm pears
5 tablespoons lemon marmalade
1 tablespoon water

Pre-heat the oven to 200°C/400°F/Gas Mark 6.

1   To make the pastry, sift the flour into a bowl and rub in the butter until the mixture resembles breadcrumbs. Stir in the sugar and egg yolks. Knead gently until smooth, then cover and chill for 30 minutes.

2   For the custard filling, mix together the sugar and eggs. Sift in the flour and mix well. In a saucepan, heat the milk to simmering point and slowly add to the egg mixture, stirring constantly. Return to the pan. Add the lemon rind and bring to the boil, stirring all the time. Simmer for 1 minute. Pour into a bowl and cover with wet greaseproof paper to prevent a skin forming. Allow to cool.

3   Roll out the pastry to fit a 25cm/10in loose-based flan tin. Trim the edges and bake blind for 20 minutes. Remove the baking weights and reduce the heat to 180°C/350°F/Gas Mark 4. Return to the oven and bake for a further 15 minutes or until the pastry is cooked. Remove from the tin and cool on a wire rack.

4 Peel, core and thinly slice the pears. Melt the lemon marmalade with the water in a saucepan, bring to the boil and brush a little over the inside of the flan. Beat the cooled custard until smooth and spoon into the flan, levelling the surface. Arrange the pear slices on top and brush all over with the lemon glaze.

Serving suggestion: Serve with cream or as it is.

Caramel Pears

Serves 4   Preparation time: 15 minutes   Cooking time: 5 minutes

The caramel sauce in this recipe is very versatile. If you have any left over, it will keep well in the refrigerator and is delicious with vanilla ice-cream or plain sponge cake.

For the caramel sauce:
50g/2oz sugar
3 tablespoons cold water
3 tablespoons hot water
350ml/12fl oz whipping cream
1 teaspoon vanilla essence
1 teaspoon unsalted butter

For the pears:
2 large ripe pears
1 lemon
2 tablespoons butter, melted
Sugar to sprinkle

---

1   Make the sauce by placing the sugar and cold water into a saucepan. Allow the sugar to dissolve over a low heat. Bring to the boil, being very careful that the mixture does not burn. Boil until the syrup turns brown.

---

2   Remove from the heat, add the hot water carefully and then the cream. Stir and return to a moderate heat to simmer until the mixture thickens (8 minutes), swirling the pan occasionally. Remove from the heat and add the vanilla and butter.

---

3   To prepare the pears, line a baking tray with foil. Peel the pears and cut in half horizontally. Remove the cores. Cut the lemon in half and rub over the pears to prevent discoloration. Score around the sides of the pears but do not cut through. Arrange the pear halves on the baking tray, brush with melted butter and sprinkle with sugar.

---

4   Place under a hot grill until golden brown (5 minutes).

Serving suggestion: Spoon the sauce on to individual plates and top with the pears. Serve immediately.

Puffed Blue Cheese Pears

Serves 6   Preparation time: 20 minutes   Cooking time: 20 minutes

Talk about versatile! You will get equally rave reviews for this recipe as a dessert.

175g/6oz frozen puff pastry, thawed
3 tablespoons butter
3 pears, peeled, cored and sliced
  5mm/¼in thick
2 tablespoons sugar
225ml/8fl oz port wine
50g/2oz mild blue cheese
(e.g. blue brie)
50g/2oz cream cheese
50g/2oz walnut pieces, toasted

Pre-heat the oven to 190°C/375°F/Gas Mark 5.
Microwave: to save time, defrost the pastry in the microwave. Simply wrap the pastry loosely in kitchen paper. Set the microwave on low power and heat for 1 minute. Allow to stand for 15 minutes before using.

1 Roll out the pastry to 5mm/¼in thick and cut into 6 rectangles, each measuring 5cm/2in × 10cm/4in. Place on an oiled baking tray and bake for 20 minutes until golden. Cool and reduce the oven temperature to 180°C/350°F/Gas Mark 4.

2 In a heavy frying pan, melt the butter and add the pears. Sprinkle with the sugar and sauté for 8 minutes until the pears are soft and the sugar caramelised. Set aside.

3 In another saucepan, boil the port wine until reduced to approximately 50ml/2floz. Split the pastry rectangles in half horizontally. Mix together the blue cheese and cream cheese and spread over the bottom half of the pastry. Add the pears, drizzle with the port and sprinkle with toasted walnuts. Top with the upper pastry halves and return to the oven for just 1 minute to warm through.

Serving suggestion: Serve warm straight from the oven.

Ham Steaks
with Fruity Pear Sauce

Serves 6   Preparation time: 10 minutes   Cooking time: 35 minutes

6 gammon steaks, 1cm/½in thick
3 large, firm pears, peeled, cored
  and sliced
425ml/¾ pint orange juice
1 tablespoon sugar
1 teaspoon wholegrain mustard
1 tablespoon cornflour
2 tablespoons water

1   Trim a little of the fat from the gammon steaks. Place the fat in a frying pan
     and heat until brown, greasing the bottom of the pan, then discard the fat.
     Make 4 or 5 snips around the fat of each steak using kitchen scissors and
     cook 2 at a time until lightly browned on each side. Remove and keep warm.

2   Add the pear slices to the pan with the orange juice, sugar and mustard. Place
     the gammon back into the pan, spooning a little sauce over the top. Simmer
     for 20 minutes. Remove the steaks to a serving dish and keep warm.

3   Mix together the cornflour and water and add to the pan juices, stirring con-
     stantly over the heat until the sauce has thickened.

Serving suggestion: Serve the sauce with the steaks.

Pear Bread and Butter Pudding

Serves 6—8   Preparation time: 15 minutes   Cooking time: 40—50 minutes

5—8 slices bread
50g/2oz butter or margarine
225g/8oz pears, peeled, cored
  and sliced
75g/3oz raisins (optional)
1 teaspoon nutmeg
700ml/1¼ pints creamy milk
150g/5oz sugar
4 eggs
1 teaspoon vanilla essence
Custard or cream to serve

Pre-heat the oven to 180°C/350°F/Gas Mark 4.
Microwave: Prepare as described in a casserole dish. Cook on power 7 for 10—13 minutes until the centre is set. Allow to stand for 1 minute before serving.

1   Lightly butter a 30 × 20cm/12 × 8in baking dish. Remove the crusts from the bread slices and butter one side generously. Cut each slice diagonally into 2 triangles and arrange half of them, butter side up, in the bottom of the baking dish. Top with half the pear slices, half the raisins if using, and a little nutmeg. Repeat this with another layer using all the remaining ingredients.

2   In a saucepan heat the milk until it just begins to bubble. Remove from the heat, add the sugar and stir until dissolved. Beat the eggs in a separate bowl and slowly stir in the hot milk. Stir in the vanilla and then pour the whole mixture over the bread triangles.

3   Set the baking dish in a tray of hot water and bake for 40—50 minutes until the pudding is cooked through. Leave for at least 10 minutes before serving.

Serving suggestion: Serve hot or cold with custard or cream.

Pear Bisque

For the soup:
3 tablespoons unsalted butter
50g/2oz onion, finely chopped
1 medium turnip, diced
2 teaspoons ground ginger
1 litre/1¾ pints chicken stock
900g/2½lb firm pears, peeled,
  cored and chopped
350ml/12fl oz whipping cream
75ml/3fl oz sherry
2 tablespoons brown sugar
½ teaspoon allspice
Salt and freshly ground white
  pepper

For the garnish:
3 firm pears, peeled, cored and
  sliced
Whipping cream

---

1   In a heavy saucepan, melt the butter and cook the onion and turnip until soft. Add the ginger and cook for a few minutes, stirring. Add the stock and bring to the boil. Add the chopped pears. Simmer half-covered for 40 minutes until the pears are very soft.

---

2   Using a blender or food processor, purée the soup and return to the saucepan. Add the cream, sherry, lemon juice, sugar, allspice and seasoning to taste. Simmer gently for a further 25 minutes, stirring occasionally. Adjust the seasoning as required.

Serving suggestion: Serve the soup garnished with slices of pear and a swirl of whipping cream.

Stuffed Pears

Serves 4—8   Preparation time: 10 minutes

Such a simple starter to prepare, this is equally delicious as a light luncheon salad.

4 large, even-sized pears
French dressing
225g/8oz cottage cheese
4 spring onions, finely chopped
100g/4oz peeled prawns
Rind of ½ lemon, finely grated
Salt and freshly ground black
  pepper
Fresh, crisp lettuce to serve

1 Peel the pears and slice them in half lengthways. Using a spoon, scoop out the core, leaving a cavity in the centre. Brush all over with a little French dressing.

2 In a bowl, combine all the remaining ingredients and season to taste. Spoon the mixture into the pear cavities.

Serving suggestion: Serve on a bed of crisp lettuce.

CHAPTER 2

AS ENGLISH AS RHUBARB AND CHERRIES

'There is a garden in her face
Where roses and white lilies grow;
A heavenly paradise is that place,
Wherein all pleasant fruits do flow,
There cherries grow which none may buy,
Til "Cherry-ripe" themselves do cry.'

So wrote Thomas Campion in the sixteenth century. How popular the cherry has become since the Romans first introduced it from Asia Minor! Always in demand for desserts and other culinary delights from the fifteenth and sixteenth centuries, cherries were also used for medicinal purposes. 'The black sowre cherries do strengthen the stomack,' wrote Langham in 1597.

Rhubarb, too, although technically considered a vegetable rather than a fruit, has seen a multitude of applications since it was used increasingly across Europe during the fourteenth century. Once cultivated for its medicinal properties by monks, and then for its ornamental qualities in sixteenth-century Germany and Italy, it is for its usefulness in puddings and pies that rhubarb has found a place in the kitchen of today. Rhubarb, in fact, reached the height of its popularity during Victorian times when the Queen herself greatly enjoyed it. Since then, varieties have changed, improved, and increased in numbers, and the wide range of recipes available gives us a wonderful opportunity to explore the versatility of both rhubarb and cherries. You may be surprised to see so many savoury dishes included here, but all it takes is the spirit of adventure to create a whole new role for these perennial favourites.

Rhubarb Pie

Serves 6—8   Preparation time: 40 minutes   Cooking time: 50—60 minutes

For the pastry:
225g/8oz flour
Pinch of salt
50g/2oz lard
50g/2oz butter
Cold water

For the filling:
2 tablespoons flour
200g/7oz light brown sugar
350g/12oz rhubarb, chopped into
  bite-sized pieces
1 lemon, peeled and very thinly
  sliced
75ml/3fl oz soured cream
75ml/3fl oz single cream to serve

Pre-heat the oven to 190°C/375°F/Gas Mark 5.

1   Make the pastry by combining the flour and salt in a bowl and cut in the lard and butter. Rub in until the mixture resembles fine breadcrumbs. Add water, 1 tablespoon at a time, until the mixture forms a stiff dough. Knead gently, cover and refrigerate for 20 minutes.

2   After 20 minutes, roll out the pastry on a lightly-floured board and use it to line a 23cm/9in pie dish. Reserve any left-over pastry for decoration.

3   To make the filling, combine the flour and the brown sugar, sprinkling a third of this over the base of the pie. Arrange a third of the chopped rhubarb on top and scatter with one third of the lemon slices. Repeat this layering until all these ingredients have been used up. If enough pastry is left over, use it to make a lattice effect on top of the pie, or cut left overs into shapes using a biscuit cutter.

4   Bake for about 50—60 minutes until the pie is golden brown and the filling cooked and juicy. Mix together the creams and serve the pie hot with this drizzled over the top.

Serving suggestion: You may wish to serve the cream separately.

Orange and Rhubarb Compote

Serves 2—4   Preparation time: 25 minutes   Chilling time: 2 hours

Here is a dessert that goes especially well with slices of Madeira cake or home-baked sweet biscuits.

1 large orange
450g/1lb fresh rhubarb, trimmed
  and chopped into 2.5cm/1in
  pieces
75g/3oz redcurrant jelly
  (see page 112)
75g/3oz orange marmalade
¼ teaspoon ground cloves
Sugar to taste
Soured cream to serve
Soft brown sugar to serve

---

1 Grate the orange rind, reserving the orange. Place the rind in a saucepan with the rhubarb, redcurrant jelly, marmalade and cloves. Cook gently for about 20 minutes until the rhubarb is soft.

---

2 Drain the rhubarb and return the liquid to the saucepan. Boil for about 5 minutes until the mixture is reduced by half. Add the rhubarb, cover and chill thoroughly.

---

3 Remove any white pith from the orange and chop the flesh. Add to the rhubarb with sugar to taste.

Serving suggestion: Spoon into individual serving bowls and top with a dollop of soured cream and a sprinkling of brown sugar.

Barbecued Lamb with Rhubarb

Serves 4   Preparation time: see below   Cooking time: see below

It is best to marinate the lamb overnight before cooking. Although this recipe gives instructions for roasting the lamb, the dish is truly magical if cooked over the hot coals of a barbecue.

1.1kg/3lb boned shoulder of
  lamb
225ml/8fl oz chicken stock
50g/2oz wholegrain mustard
50ml/2fl oz soy sauce
2 tablespoons lemon juice
2 tablespoons fresh thyme
6 small onions, finely chopped
1 clove garlic
Oil to rub
Salt and freshly ground black
  pepper
450ml/16fl oz water
50g/2oz sugar
225g/8oz rhubarb, chopped
225ml/8fl oz vegetable oil
50ml/2fl oz red wine vinegar
Curly endive to garnish

1   Place the lamb in a roasting tin. Mix together the stock, mustard, soy sauce, lemon juice, thyme, onion and garlic. Pour this mixture over the lamb. Marinate in the refrigerator overnight, basting occasionally.

Pre-heat the oven to 230°C/450°F/Gas Mark 8.

2   Remove the lamb from the marinade and reserve. Rub the lamb with the oil, salt and pepper and roast for 30 minutes. Then reduce the heat to 180°C/350°F/Gas Mark 4 and continue cooking for 30 minutes per 450g/1lb, or until the lamb is crisp on the outside and slightly pink on the inside.

3   Whilst the lamb is cooking, heat the 450ml/16fl oz water and sugar in the saucepan until the sugar dissolves and then add the rhubarb. Simmer until the rhubarb is soft and leave to cool. Drain.

4   Bring the reserved marinade to the boil. Strain and then beat in the oil and vinegar.

Serving suggestion: Serve the lamb sliced on to individual dishes and surround with the rhubarb. Pour the marinade over the top and garnish with the curly endive.

Rhubarb Bavarian with Strawberry Sauce

Serves 6   Preparation time: 30 minutes   Cooking time: 5 minutes

For the Rhubarb Bavarian:
*450g/1lb rhubarb, trimmed and
  sliced*
75g/3oz sugar
2 tablespoons water
*11g/½oz sachet powdered
  gelatine, dissolved in 2
  tablespoons hot water*
2 egg whites
2 tablespoons sugar
*175ml/6fl oz double cream,
  whipped*
Fresh strawberries to garnish

For the strawberry sauce:
350g/12oz strawberries, hulled
75g/3oz sugar
2 tablespoons white wine

1   In a saucepan combine the rhubarb, sugar and water. Place over a medium heat and cook until the rhubarb is soft. Mash thoroughly with a fork and allow to cool. Add the dissolved gelatine to the rhubarb and stir until combined. Chill until syrupy.

2   Beat the egg whites, gradually adding the 2 tablespoons of sugar until stiff. Fold into the rhubarb mixture. Fold in the whipped cream. Spoon the mixture into an 850ml/1½ pint mould and chill until firm.

3   To make the sauce, place the strawberries, sugar and wine into a blender or food processor and blend to a thick, smooth purée. Press through a fine sieve to remove any seeds.

Serving suggestion: Remove the Rhubarb Bavarian from the mould and garnish with fresh strawberries. Serve the sauce separately.

Rhubarb and Raspberry Soup

Serves 4—6   Preparation time: 20 minutes

For a refreshing first course or summer dessert try substituting the raspberries with strawberries.

275g/10oz raspberries, hulled
450g/1lb rhubarb, trimmed
300ml/11fl oz fresh orange juice
100g/4oz sugar
1 orange, peeled and chopped
Natural yoghurt to serve

1   Place all but 8 of the raspberries into a saucepan, reserving the rest for the garnish. Chop the rhubarb into small pieces and add to the raspberries. Add the fresh orange juice and bring to the boil. Simmer, uncovered, for about 1 minute and then remove from the heat and allow to cool.

2   Add the sugar, adjusting to taste. Using a blender or food processor, purée the mixture and then pass it through a fine sieve to remove any seeds. Pour into a large bowl, add the chopped orange, cover and chill.

Serving suggestion: Serve the soup garnished with the reserved raspberries and a swirl of yoghurt on the top.

Rhubarb Ice-cream with Crunch Topping

Serve 4—6   Preparation time: 20 minutes   Freezing time: 4 hours

For the ice-cream:
450g/1lb rhubarb, trimmed
150ml/¼ pint water
100g/4oz sugar to taste
2 teaspoons lemon juice
1 teaspoon ground ginger
1 egg white
275ml/½ pint double cream

For the topping:
75g/3oz wholemeal breadcrumbs
75g/3oz brown sugar
1 teaspoon mixed spice

1   Chop the rhubarb into bite-sized pieces and place in a saucepan with the water and sugar. Adjust the quantity of sugar to suit your taste. Cook gently until the rhubarb is tender and allow to cool. Add the lemon juice and transfer to a freezer container. Freeze until the mixture begins to set around the edges.

2   Scoop the mixture into a bowl and beat thoroughly until smooth. Then add the ginger. Whip the egg white until stiff and fold into the rhubarb. Beat the cream until thick and fold in. Return to the freezer container and place in the freezer. Leave to freeze solid, interrupting twice with a good mixing to keep the ice-cream smooth.

3   Meanwhile, make the topping. Mix together the topping ingredients in a bowl. Spread out on a sheet of foil and place under a hot grill. Mix under the heat until crisp and crunchy. Allow to cool.

Serving suggestion: Allow the ice-cream to soften slightly before scooping out into individual bowls. Serve sprinkled with the crunchy topping and with home-made sweet biscuits.

Rhubarb Shortbread Layer

Serves 4—6   Preparation time: 20 minutes   Cooking time: 15 minutes

This is a very pretty dessert when served in individual parfait glasses. Of course, you can make your own shortbread, but shop-bought all-butter shortbread is equally good.

450g/1lb rhubarb, trimmed
75—100g/3—4oz sugar to taste
2 tablespoons water
Grated rind of 1 orange
225g/8oz shortbread biscuits
575ml/1 pint double cream
Brown sugar to sprinkle

Microwave: To cook the rhubarb in the microwave, simply chop it as directed and place in a covered dish with the 2 tablespoons water, the sugar and orange rind. Cook on high power for 9—10 minutes. Leave to stand for 5 minutes and then put aside to cool.

1   Chop the rhubarb into bite-sized pieces. Place the sugar and water in a saucepan and heat until the sugar is completely dissolved. Add the rhubarb and orange rind and simmer gently, uncovered, until the rhubarb is soft but still holds its shape. Put aside to cool completely.

2   Using a rolling pin, crush the shortbread to fairly large crumbs. Whip the double cream until thick.

3   Take 4 or 6 parfait glasses and spoon some of the rhubarb into the bottom of each. Make a layer with some of the crushed biscuits and top with some cream. Repeat the layers until all the rhubarb and biscuits are used up, finishing with a layer of cream on top.

Serving suggestion: Sprinkle with a little brown sugar and serve chilled.

Sweet Cherry Soup

Serves 6   Preparation time: 10 minutes   Chilling time: 4 hours

You will be really surprised at just how easy this soup is to make — and it's so tasty you can serve it any time.

450g/1lb cherries, stoned
125ml/4fl oz cherry juice
125ml/4fl oz single cream
125ml/4fl oz natural yoghurt
1 teaspoon grated orange rind
Pinch of cinnamon
1 orange, peeled and thinly
    sliced to garnish

1   In a blender or food processor combine the first 6 ingredients until smooth.

2   Pour into a large serving dish, cover and chill thoroughly.

Serving suggestion: Serve garnished with the slices of orange floating on the top.

Indian Fruit Rice with Pine Nuts

Serves 4   Preparation time: 30 minutes   Cooking time: 50 minutes

This makes a lovely dish on its own, but its colour and refreshing tastes are especially suited to accompany a roast leg of lamb.

250g/9oz basmati rice or Indian long-grain rice
1.7 litres/3 pints water
Salt to season
25ml/1fl oz vegetable oil
4 cardamom pods
4 whole cloves
1 bay-leaf
2.5cm/1in cinnamon stick

1 onion, thinly sliced
225g/8oz soft fruits, e.g. cherries, apricots, peaches, raspberries, oranges and grapes, peeled and chopped
1 teaspoon sugar
25g/1oz roasted pine nuts or almonds

1   Rinse the rice thoroughly under cold water, then place in a bowl just covered with water. Leave to soak for 30 minutes. Drain.

2   In a large saucepan bring the 1.7 litres/3 pints water to the boil. Add the rice, mix and boil for 5 minutes. Drain thoroughly and return the rice to the saucepan. Season with salt. Cover and put aside.

3   Heat the oil in a heavy-based frying pan and add the cardamom pods, cloves, bay-leaf and cinnamon. Cook for 15 seconds and then add the onion. Stir until the onion lightly browns (5 minutes). Add the fruit, increase the heat and cook until the fruit is cooked through. Sprinkle with the sugar and cook until the sugar melts.

4   Fold the fruit into the rice and sprinkle with the nuts. Serve hot or cold.

Serving suggestion: Serve with roast leg of lamb.

No-bake Cherry Cheesecake

Serves 8—10   Preparation time: 1½ hours

For the base and filling:
1 quantity biscuit crust
  (see page 25)
550g/1¼lb cottage cheese
2 x 11g/½oz sachets powdered
  gelatine
50g/2oz sugar
¼ teaspoon salt
2 large eggs, separated
225ml/8fl oz milk
1 teaspoon grated lemon rind
2 tablespoons lemon juice
1 teaspoon vanilla essence
2 tablespoons icing sugar
¼ teaspoon cream of tartar
225ml/8fl oz double cream,
  whipped

For the cherry topping:
450g/1lb cherries, stoned and
  halved
50ml/2fl oz water
50g/2oz sugar
1 tablespoon cornflour
1 teaspoon lemon juice

1   Make the biscuit crust as directed (see page 25) and line a 23cm/9in pie dish with it. Chill in the refrigerator.

2   Press the cottage cheese through a sieve into a bowl and drain off any excess liquid. In a saucepan, mix the gelatine, sugar and salt together and gently beat in the egg yolks and milk. Bring to the boil, stirring, and put to one side. Add the lemon rind, lemon juice and vanilla essence and allow to cool.

3   In a large bowl, add the cottage cheese to the gelatine mixture and leave in the refrigerator to chill, stirring occasionally.

4   Beat the egg whites until stiff and gradually add the icing sugar and cream of tartar, beating continually. Fold into the cottage cheese mixture and then fold in the whipped cream. Pour into the prepared crust and chill thoroughly before adding the cherry topping.

5   To make the topping, place the cherries, water and sugar into a saucepan, bring to the boil and simmer gently until the cherries soften and the juices run. Strain and reserve the juice. In a small bowl mix together the cornflour with 1 tablespoon sugar and the lemon juice. Add 125ml/4fl oz of cherry syrup, made up with water if necessary. Stir to the boil and continue to boil until thick and clear. Remove from the heat, add the cherries and leave to cool to room temperature. Pour on top of the cheesecake, return to the refrigerator and leave to set.

Serving suggestion: If you like, serve with additional single cream.

Note: You may use bottled cherries for the topping. Just drain and use the bottled syrup as directed.

Duck with Cherries

Serves 4   Preparation time: 20 minutes   Cooking time: see below

The rich meat of the duck goes particularly well with the sweet, ripe cherries.

1 oven-ready duck
Butter and salt for roasting
275ml/½ pint stock
3 sugar lumps
1 orange

40g/1½oz sugar
1 wineglass port
450g/1lb red cherries, stoned
575ml/1 pint rich gravy

Pre-heat the oven to 190°C 375°F/Gas Mark 5.

Microwave: The duck can easily be roasted in the microwave. Place the bird breastside down on to a roasting rack and pierce the skin under the legs. Rub the duck with the butter and salt and brush with the stock. Cover loosely with a slit roasting bag. Cook for 8 minutes per 450g/1lb on power 7. Half-way through the cooking time, drain off any excess juices. Remove the roasting bag for the last 8—10 minutes. Drain off the juices, cover the duck with foil and leave for 6 minutes.

---

1   Rub the duck with the butter and sprinkle with the salt. Place in a roasting pan with the stock and cook for 30 minutes per 450g/1lb, basting occasionally. The duck should still be slightly pink when cooked.

---

2   Rub the sugar lumps over the skin of the orange and place them in a saucepan with the rest of the sugar and the port. Add the juice from the orange and heat until the sugar has dissolved. Add the cherries and simmer gently for about 5 minutes until the cherries are just tender. Drain the cherries but keep them warm and reserve the syrup.

---

3   Remove the duck from the oven and cut into quarters. Place on a serving dish and keep warm.

---

4   Combine the cherry syrup with the hot gravy and mix together thoroughly. Spoon half the sauce over the duck and top with the warm cherries. Serve the remaining sauce separately.

Serving suggestion: Serve with freshly cooked vegetables. Use your own favourite gravy for this recipe — the richer and more highly flavoured, the deeper and tastier the sauce.

Duck and Cherry Mousse

Serves 8   Preparation time: 30 minutes   Setting time: 4 hours

You may like to substitute chicken for the duck in this recipe — or part chicken and part ham. In any combination it's delicious!

1½ tablespoons powdered
  gelatine
50ml/2fl oz cold chicken stock
125ml/4fl oz hot chicken stock
3 egg yolks
350ml/12fl oz milk
450g/1lb duck, minced and
  cooked
150g/5oz cherries, stoned and
  halved
Salt and freshly ground white
  pepper
Paprika
225ml/8fl oz whipping cream
Crisp lettuce to serve
Whole cherries to garnish

---

1   Soak the gelatine in the cold stock for about 5 minutes, then add the hot stock and leave while the gelatine thoroughly dissolves.

---

2   In a small bowl beat the egg yolks and add the milk. Set over a pan of simmering water and cook, stirring constantly, until the mixture is smooth and fairly thick. Stir in the gelatine mixture and allow to cool. Add the minced duck, cherries and season with the salt, pepper and a dash of paprika.

---

3   Chill in the refrigerator until almost set and then fold in the whipping cream. Spoon the mixture into a dampened jelly mould and leave in the refrigerator to set.

Serving suggestion: Serve turned out on to a serving dish with fresh crisp lettuce leaves. Garnish with whole cherries.

Cherry Cream Crêpes

Serves 4   Preparation time: 1 ½ hours

What a wonderful combination of summer fruit flavours!

For the crêpes:
100g/4oz plain flour
Pinch of salt
Grated rind of ½ lemon
1 egg
275ml/½ pint milk
15g/½oz melted butter
butter for frying

For the cherry cream:
450g/1lb cherries, stoned
150ml/¼ pint whipping or
  double cream
225g/8oz cream cheese
2 tablespoons kirsch

For the raspberry sauce:
225g/8oz raspberries, hulled
Icing sugar to taste
Dash of kirsch (optional)

1   To prepare the crêpes, sift the flour and salt together in a bowl. Add the lemon rind and break the egg into the centre. Add the milk slowly, beating well to keep the batter smooth. Add the melted butter and beat well.

2   Heat a very little extra butter in a heavy-based frying pan to coat the bottom and when very hot pour in enough batter to coat the base thinly. Cook until golden brown underneath and then turn or toss quickly to cook the other side. Repeat until all the batter is used up. Stack the pancakes between pieces of greaseproof paper and keep warm.

3   To make the cherry cream, purée the cherries in a blender or food processor and then pass through a fine sieve to remove any skin. Whip the cream and cream cheese until thick and then fold in the cherries and kirsch. Cover and keep in the refrigerator whilst making the raspberry sauce.

4 In a blender or food processor, purée the respberries and then pass through a fine sieve to remove the seeds. Add enough icing sugar to suit your taste and a dash of kirsch if using.

Serving suggestion: To serve this dessert, fill the crêpes with the cherry cream and arrange on a serving dish. Trickle over half the raspberry sauce and serve the remaining sauce separately.

Cherry Meringue

Serves 8   Preparation time: 30 minutes   Cooking time: 4½—5 hours

'...goddess, nymph, perfect, divine!
To what, my love, shall I compare thine eyne?
Crystal is muddy. O! how ripe in show
Thy lips, those kissing cherries, tempting grow...'
                              William Shakespeare,
                              A Midsummer Night's Dream

4 egg whites
225g/8oz caster sugar
450g/1lb ripe cherries
1 tablespoon kirsch
425ml/¾ pint whipping cream

Pre-heat the oven to 110°C/225°F/Gas Mark ¼.

---

1   Prepare 2 baking trays by lining with non-stick parchment paper, and mark
     with a pencil a 20cm/8in circle on each. In a bowl whisk the egg whites until
     stiff. Add the sugar 1 tablespoon at a time, whisking well until half the sugar
     is used. Fold in the remaining sugar with a metal spoon.

---

2   Spread half the mixture within the circle on one tray and place the remainder
     in a piping bag fitted with a plain nozzle. Pipe around the outer ring of the
     other circle. Pipe a lattice pattern across the circle and pipe another circle
     on top of the original one. Place in the oven for 4½—5 hours until the mer-
     ingue is thoroughly dry. Allow to cool before removing the paper.

---

3   Wash the cherries and reserve some for decoration. Remove the stones, cut
     in half and place in a bowl with the kirsch. Mix well. Meanwhile whip
     275ml/½pint of the cream and fold in the soaked cherries. Spread over the
     flat meringue base. Place the lattice meringue on top. Whip the remaining
     cream and, using a piping bag fitted with a star-shaped nozzle, pipe around
     the top.

Serving suggestion: Serve decorated with the reserved cherries.

Note: The meringue rounds can be made in advance and stored for several weeks
in an airtight container.

Cherry Salad Mould

Serves 6—8   Preparation time: 30 minutes   Setting time: 2—3 hours

Serve this attractive moulded salad on a bed of crisp lettuce and you will have an excellent dish for any buffet table.

75g/3oz cherry-flavoured gelatine
225ml/8fl oz boiling water
175ml/6fl oz sherry
450g/1lb cherries, stoned
100g/4oz almonds or pecans,
  chopped
75g/3oz packet cream cheese,
  cubed
Crisp lettuce to serve
Fresh mint leaves to garnish

1   In a small bowl dissolve the gelatine with the boiling water. Stir in the sherry and leave in the refrigerator until thickened to the consistency of egg white.

2   When thickened, add the cherries and nuts, and then the cream cheese. Mix in thoroughly. Pour the mixture into a 1 litre/1¾ pint ring mould and refrigerate for 2—3 hours until firm.

Serving suggestion: To serve, release from the mould on to a dish lined with lettuce leaves and garnish with the fresh mint leaves.

CHAPTER 3

THE BERRY PATCH

Somehow, when we first see succulent strawberries and raspberries being sold on the market stall or along the roadside with pots of thick cream, or pick-your-own signs appearing at farm gates, we know that it is the beginning of long, lazy summer days, picnics in the countryside and weekends by the sea. Perhaps more than any other fruit, these are the berries which signify that summer is really here at last!

Today, as in the sixteenth century, we may still find berries such as the blackberry growing wild in the hedgerows and woods, and what a lovely excuse it is for a family expedition to fill baskets with these hand-picked delights. Some fruits, such as the elderberry and rowan-berry, remain undoubtedly a wild harvest, whereas other native wild plants, such as the cranberry and blueberry, have been taken into gardens and brought under cultivation. The gooseberry has been a popular favourite for centuries and is put to a huge variety of uses, yet it is little eaten anywhere in the world other than in Britain. We rarely see the small wild strawberry in gardens today, where the larger and rather sweeter domestic variety reigns. Once grown for both medicinal purposes and as dessert fruits, both the strawberry and the raspberry represent the best of nature's abundance. So agreed Dr William Butler, who wrote in the seventeenth century: 'Doubtless God could have made a better berry; but doubtless God never did.'

Sadly, it is not possible to mention all the many different berries, but I hope that this wide range of recipes encourages you to discover the great versatility of these delicious fruits.

Strawberry and Raspberry Soufflé

Serves 8—10   Preparation time: 45 minutes   Chilling time: overnight

A wonderful way to combine two favourite summer fruits. This soufflé is eye-catching and looks far more difficult than it really is. It is best made the night before you plan to serve it.

For the soufflé:
225g/8oz strawberries, hulled
225g/8oz raspberries, hulled
11g/½oz sachet powdered
  gelatine
2 tablespoons water
2 tablespoons lemon juice
100g/4oz caster sugar
4 eggs, separated
275ml/½ pint whipping cream

For the decoration:
50g/2oz toasted almonds, finely
  chopped
150ml/¼ pint whipping cream,
  whipped
4—6 fresh strawberries, halved
8 whole hazelnuts

---

1   First prepare a 1.1 litre/2 pint soufflé dish by wrapping a double band of greaseproof paper around the dish, to stand about 5cm/2in above the rim. Secure with string.

---

2   In a blender or food processor, thoroughly purée the strawberries and raspberries then pass through a fine sieve and reserve. In a small bowl sprinkle the gelatine over the water and lemon juice and allow to soften, then place the bowl over a pan of simmering water until the gelatine has dissolved. Leave to cool but do not allow to set.

---

3   In another bowl set over a pan of simmering water put the sugar and egg yolks. Remove the pan from the heat and whisk the mixture until creamy, thick and light. Remove the bowl from the pan and continue whisking until cold. Add the berry purée and gelatine, stir together and leave until just beginning to set.

4   Whisk the egg whites until stiff and fold into the gelatine mixture. Whip the cream until soft and thick and fold into the mixture. Pour into the prepared soufflé dish and chill in the refrigerator overnight.

Serving suggestion: Very carefully remove the band of greaseproof paper using a knife and press the chopped almonds around the side. Decorate the top of the soufflé with whipped cream, halved strawberries and hazelnuts.

Strawberry Fool with Raspberry Sauce

Serves 4   Preparation time: 25 minutes

For the fool:
450g/1lb fresh strawberries
2 tablespoons honey
Grated rind of ½ lemon
300ml/½ pint double cream
3 tablespoons sherry (optional)

For the sauce:
225g/8oz raspberries, hulled
60g/2½oz icing sugar
150ml/¼ pint whipping cream,
  whipped
Fresh raspberries to decorate

---

1 Using a blender or food processor, thoroughly purée the strawberries and then pass through a fine sieve. Mix in the honey and lemon rind. Whip the cream until thick and fold in the fruit purée. Add the sherry if desired. Divide into 4 individual glass dishes and chill in the refrigerator whilst making the sauce.

---

2 To make the sauce, purée the raspberries, then pass them through a fine sieve. Stir in the icing sugar until dissolved. Whip the cream and place a spoonful on top of each fool. Decorate with the fresh raspberries.

Serving suggestion: Drizzle some sauce over the top with the remaining sauce served separately.

Strawberry and Spinach Salad

Serves 4—6   Preparation time: 10 minutes

This really is an easy salad to 'toss up' as either a starter, an accompaniment to a main course, or as a lovely luncheon dish served with crispy French bread.

75ml/3fl oz vegetable oil
3 tablespoons red wine vinegar
2 teaspoons fresh lemon juice
1 teaspoon grated fresh ginger
450g/1lb fresh spinach, trimmed
175g/6oz strawberries, hulled
   and sliced
100g/4oz Cheddar cheese, grated

1 Make the salad dressing by combining the oil, vinegar, lemon juice and ginger. Mix well.

2 Place the spinach, strawberries and cheese in a large bowl. Pour over the dressing and toss thoroughly.

Serving suggestion: Serve immediately.

Dipped Strawberries with Soured Cream

Serves 6—8   Preparation time: 30 minutes

This simple but luxurious dessert is always a conversation piece at the dinner table.

450g/1lb fresh strawberries with
  stems
350g/¾lb plain chocolate
Soured cream to serve

1   Rinse the strawberries under cold running water and pat dry with kitchen paper. Be careful not to remove the stems. Keep at room temperature. Lay out sheets of greaseproof paper on a flat surface. Place the chocolate in a saucepan set over a pan of boiling water and melt until completely smooth. Replace the boiling water with cold water and set the saucepan of melted chocolate over the top.

2   Allow the chocolate to cool slightly, stirring constantly. Keep the chocolate at a good dipping consistency while you work with it. Dip each strawberry into the chocolate, leaving a small part uncovered. Hold each one over the pan to allow any excess to drip off. Place the dipped fruit on the greaseproof paper and leave to dry and set. Keep in the refrigerator until ready to serve.

Serving suggestion: Place the dipped fruit on a large serving dish in the centre of the table. Serve each person with an individual bowl of soured cream. Take a strawberry from the centre, dip in the soured cream and... simply delicious.

Little Berry Pizzas

Serves 6   Preparation time: 25 minutes   Cooking time: 20 minutes

These little pastries are best eaten straight from the oven. If fresh berries are not available, you can use frozen ones, but thaw and drain them before weighing them. You'll fall in love with this rich buttery pastry and, of course, you can use any variety of soft fruits for the filling.

For the pastry:
200g/7oz unsalted butter
50g/2oz sugar
1 egg
1 teaspoon lemon rind, grated
25g/1oz ground almonds, lightly
  toasted
225g/8oz plain flour
1 teaspoon baking powder

For the filling:
100g/4oz blueberries
6 tablespoons sugar
2 teaspoons cornflour
100g/4oz raspberries or
  strawberries, hulled
Whipped cream to serve

---

1   First make the pastry . Using a blender or food processor, cream the butter with the sugar until light and fluffy. Add the egg and lemon rind and mix thoroughly.

---

2   Combine the ground almonds with 2 tablespoons of the flour. Mix together the remaining flour with the baking powder, add to the mixture with the ground almonds and then combine well with the butter mixture. Wrap in clingfilm and chill thoroughly.

---

3   Line a baking tray with greaseproof paper. Divide the pastry into 6 equal quantities and roll each into a 15cm/6in circle. Place on the baking tray and fold up the edges to form a border. Chill whilst making the fillings.

Pre-heat the oven to 200°C/400°F/Gas Mark 6.

---

4   In one bowl combine the blueberries with 3 tablespoons sugar and 1 teaspoon cornflour. In another bowl combine the raspberries or strawberries with the same quantity of sugar and cornflour. Fill 3 crusts with each mixture. Bake for 15—20 minutes until golden brown.

Serving suggestion: These pizzas may be served whole or sliced into quarters. Serve with whipped cream.

Marinated Chicken with Raspberry Sauce

Serves 6   Preparation time: 2½ hours   Cooking time: 35 minutes

This sauce is also delicious served with duck.

For the marinated chicken:
6 chicken breasts, skinned
225ml/8fl oz olive oil
50ml/2fl oz red wine vinegar
50g/2oz raspberries, chopped
1 tablespoon black peppercorns,
  crushed
1 teaspoon salt
2 cloves garlic, crushed
2 bay-leaves
2 sprigs fresh thyme

For the raspberry sauce:
225g/8oz raspberries
1 onion, chopped
1 tablespoon oil
4 teaspoons red wine vinegar
2 teaspoons lemon juice
3 sprigs fresh mint, finely
  chopped
Freshly ground black pepper

Pre-heat the oven to 180°C/350°F/Gas Mark 4.

1   Place the chicken breasts in a roasting pan. Combine all the marinade ingredients and pour over the chicken. Leave for 2 hours, basting occasionally. Remove the chicken from the marinade.

2   To prepare the raspberry sauce, reserve 12 raspberries for garnish and chop the remaining fruit. Fry the onion in the oil until slightly soft. Mix all the sauce ingredients together, season to taste and cook gently for 1 minute.

3   Roast the chicken pieces for 35 minutes until cooked through.

Serving suggestion: Serve garnished with the reserved raspberries. Serve the sauce separately.

Raspberry Salad

Serves 6—8   Preparation time: 30 minutes   Chilling time: 2 hours

This salad is wonderfully rich and goes especially well with a main course of beef.

1 large tin crushed pineapple in
  syrup
1 packet raspberry-flavoured
  jelly
225g/8oz raspberries, hulled
425ml/¾ pint soured cream
Crisp lettuce to serve

1   Drain the pineapple and reserve the syrup. Make the jelly according to the instructions on the packet, making up the amount of water required with the pineapple syrup. Place in a bowl and refrigerate until slightly thickened.

2   Add the pineapple and raspberries to the liquid mixture and combine thoroughly. Spoon half the mixture into a jelly ring mould. Spoon over the soured cream and then add the rest of the fruit mixture. Chill until firm.

Serving suggestion: To serve, turn out on to a serving dish lined with lettuce leaves.

Note: Be careful to measure the liquid accurately as this salad may prove a little difficult to set.

Blackberry Fool

Serves 4   Cooking time: 30 minutes   Cooling time: 15 minutes

*'If reasons were as plentie as black-berries, I would give no man
a reason upon compulsion.'*

William Shakespeare, Henry VI

450g/1lb fresh blackberries
100g/4oz sugar
4 tablespoons water
275ml/½ pint whipping cream

---

1   Reserve 4 whole blackberries for garnish. Place the remaining blackberries, sugar and water in a saucepan and bring to the boil. Cover and cook until thickened (30 minutes).

---

2   Press through a fine sieve and allow to cool. Whip the cream until thick and fold in the blackberry purée.

Serving suggestion: Spoon into individual dishes and garnish with the reserved blackberries.

Blackberry Steamed Pudding

Serves 4—6   Preparation time: 30 minutes   Cooking time: 1½ hours

25g/1oz fresh white breadcrumbs
225g/8oz self-raising flour, sieved
100g/4oz shredded suet
125ml/4fl oz water
350g/12oz fresh blackberries
1½ tablespoons caster sugar
Custard or cream to serve

Microwave: Microwaves are superb for cooking suet or steamed puddings, especially this recipe which can be cooked in just 10 minutes. Prepare as directed, although you need only cover the basin with greased greaseproof paper. Cook on high power for 5 minutes, then turn the basin and cook for another 5 minutes. It may be necessary to remove some of the juices during cooking. Remove the cover and allow the pudding to stand for about 4 minutes before serving piping hot.

---

1   In a bowl mix together the breadcrumbs, flour and suet. Add the water and bind together. Divide this mixture into 5 equal pieces and roll out each one, gradually increasing in size to fit as layers in the pudding basin.

---

2   Grease a 1.1 litre/2 pint pudding basin and place the smallest round in the bottom. Place some blackberries on top, sprinkle with a little sugar and continue layering, finishing with the largest pudding round on top. Cover the basin with greased greaseproof paper and a piece of foil, pleated to allow for expansion. Secure with string. Place in a steamer and steam steadily for 1½ hours.

Serving suggestion: Turn out and serve hot with custard or cream.

Blueberry and Lemon Curd Tart

Serves 6—8   Cooking time: 1¼ hours   Chilling time: 1½ hours

1 quantity pastry (see page 99)

For the lemon curd:
175g/6oz caster sugar
Grated rind and juice of 2
  lemons
4 eggs
100g/4oz unsalted butter, cut into
  pieces

For the blueberry topping:
50g/2oz sugar
1 tablespoon cornflour
125ml/4fl oz water
1½ teaspoons fresh lemon juice
175g/6oz fresh blueberries

Pre-heat the oven to 200°C/400°F/Gas Mark 6.

Microwave: To make the lemon curd, remember that lemons will give more juice and zest if first heated in the microwave on high power for 1 minute. Put the sugar, lemon rind, juice and butter into a casserole and cook on power 7 for 10 minutes, allowing the sugar to dissolve and the mixture to come to the boil. Add the eggs and cook for a further 6 minutes on power 7 until the mixture thickens.

1   First make the pastry as directed. Use it to line a 25cm/10in pie plate. Line the base with foil or greaseproof paper, filling with baking weights before baking blind for 20 minutes. Then remove the paper and weights, prick the base with a fork and return to the oven to bake for a further 5 minutes until golden brown. Allow to cool.

2   To make the lemon curd, place the sugar and lemon rind in a bowl. In a separate bowl whisk together the lemon juice and eggs, then add the sugar mixture. Add the butter. Place the bowl over a saucepan of simmering water and stir constantly until the mixture has thickened and will coat the spoon (20 minutes). Do not allow the mixture to boil. Cover and refrigerate for at least 1 hour.

3   Spread the lemon curd over the base of the cooled flan. In a saucepan combine the sugar and cornflour. Add the water and lemon juice and bring to the boil. Simmer, stirring constantly until the mixture thickens and turns translucent. Remove from the heat and add the blueberries, mixing well. Using a slotted spoon, arrange the blueberries over the flan and refrigerate for 30 minutes before serving.

Serving suggestion: Serve with cream.

Freezing: The lemon curd will keep for up to 1 week if covered and kept in the refrigerator.

Blueberry and Nectarine Stuffed Chicken

Serves 6—8   Preparation time: 30 minutes   Cooking time: 1 hour 20 minutes

A superb dinner-party dish. This very unusual stuffing for chicken makes such a colourful combination and is always an unexpected treat.

For the stuffed chicken:
3 tablespoons unsalted butter
2 tablespoons crushed thyme
4 firm nectarines, cut into
  eighths
175g/6oz blueberries, fresh or
  frozen
1 tablespoon lemon juice
2 x 1.1kg/3lb chickens
Butter for roasting
Salt and freshly ground black
  pepper

For the glaze:
75ml/3fl oz runny honey
50ml/2fl oz lemon juice
1 teaspoon mustard powder

Pre-heat the oven to 200°C/400°F/Gas Mark 6.

1   In a heavy frying pan melt the butter and add the thyme. If fresh thyme is not available, use 1 teaspoon dried. Add the nectarines and sauté gently for about 3 minutes, but do not allow them to turn brown. Put aside in a bowl and allow to cool.

2   Add the blueberries and lemon juice to the nectarines and stuff the chickens with this mixture. Place in a roasting tin and rub all over with a little butter. Season with salt and pepper and roast for 20 minutes.

3   After this time, remove the chickens from the oven and reduce the heat to 180°C/350°F/Gas Mark 4. In a small saucepan, mix together the honey, lemon juice and mustard and warm to a thin consistency. Baste the chickens with this mixture, return to the oven and cook for a further 1 hour, basting every 15 minutes until the chickens are cooked and all the glaze used.

4 Allow the chickens to cool at room temperature, basting occasionally with the juices.

Serving suggestion: These chickens can be served already carved, or whole and carved at the table.

Variations: Instead of nectarines, try using firm peaches and, if blueberries are hard to find, try bilberries. Bottled berries may be used but be sure to drain off the sweetened juice first.

Turkey and Cranberry Pie

Serves 6—8   Preparation time: 40 minutes   Cooking time: 30—35 minutes

This pie is perfect for using up left-over turkey or chicken, especially around Christmas time.

40g/1½oz butter or margarine
1 large onion, thinly sliced
100g/4oz mushrooms, sliced
225g/8oz fresh cranberries
40g/1½oz flour
575ml/1 pint chicken stock
Salt and freshly ground black
  pepper
675g/1½lb cooked turkey or
  chicken meat, cut into
  bite-sized pieces
1 tablespoon freshly chopped
  parsley
375g/13oz packet frozen puff
  pastry, thawed
Beaten egg or milk to glaze

Pre-heat the oven to 220°C/425°F/Gas Mark 7.

---

1   In a saucepan, melt the butter and add the onion, mushrooms and cranberries and fry gently, stirring for 5 minutes. Stir in the flour and cook for 1 minute. Gradually add the stock and seasoning to taste, bring to the boil and simmer covered for 15—20 minutes until the cranberries are tender. Add the turkey or chicken meat and parsley and mix well. Spoon into a 1.7 litre/3 pint pie dish. Allow to cool.

2   Roll out the pastry to 5cm/2in larger than the pie dish and cover the pie. Dampen the rim of the dish, trim and flute the edges. Use any remaining pastry to decorate the top. Brush with beaten egg or milk and make a hole in the centre to allow the steam to escape.

3   Bake for 15 minutes and then reduce the heat to 180°C/350°F/Gas Mark 4 and continue to cook for a further 25—30 minutes or until the pastry is golden brown.

Serving suggestion: This pie may be served hot or cold.

Freezing: Allow the pie to cool and then wrap in foil. It may be kept for up to 2 months in the freezer. To serve, thaw for several hours at room temperature. Re-heat covered with foil at 180°C/350°F/Gas Mark 4 for 45 minutes.

Cranberry Soup

This soup is served cold and can be prepared the day before serving.

500g/1lb 2oz fresh cranberries
1 litre/1¾ pints water
2 whole cloves
275g/10oz sugar
1 heaped tablespoon plain flour
500ml/18fl oz soured cream
350ml/12fl oz red wine
350ml/12fl oz fresh orange juice
Thick Greek yoghurt and fresh
  mint to serve

1   Simmer the cranberries, water and cloves in a saucepan for 10 minutes. Strain the cranberries, discarding the cloves and reserving 225ml/8fl oz of the juice. Using a blender or food processor, purée the cranberries and then press through a fine sieve into a large saucepan. Add the reserved juice.

2   In a bowl mix together the sugar and flour. Add the soured cream, wine and orange juice. Mix well and add to the cranberry purée. Bring slowly to the boil and simmer gently, stirring constantly for about 2 minutes. Cool and refrigerate until thoroughly chilled.

Serving suggestion: Serve garnished with Greek yoghurt and fresh mint.

Cranberry Bread

Serves 8—10   Preparation time: 35 minutes   Cooking time: 1 hour

This rather festive bread is irresistible straight from the oven but is wonderful any time of the day, including breakfast.

225g/8oz plain flour
½ teaspoon salt
1½ teaspoons baking powder
½ teaspoon bicarbonate of soda
200g/7oz sugar
Grated rind and juice of 1
  orange
2 tablespoons melted butter
Boiling water
1 egg, beaten
100g/4oz cranberries, chopped
100g/4oz walnuts, chopped

Pre-heat the oven to 190°C/375°F/Gas Mark 5.

1   Sift the dry ingredients together into a bowl. Combine the orange rind, orange juice and melted butter in a measuring jug and add enough boiling water to make up the quantity to 175ml/6fl oz.

2   Add the liquid to the flour mixture with the beaten egg and mix well. Add the cranberries and nuts and combine well. Pour the mixture into a greased 450g/1lb loaf tin and leave to stand for 20 minutes. Bake for 1 hour or until the bread is cooked.

Serving suggestion: Serve sliced warm or cold and spread with butter.

Freezing: This bread freezes very well. Allow to cool and wrap in foil. Seal in a freezer bag and freeze. The bread will keep for up to 6 months.

Cranberry Salad Mould

Serves 10—12   Preparation time: 25 minutes   Chilling time: 6—8 hours

This brightly-coloured moulded salad is ideal as part of a summer buffet or barbecue.

450g/1lb fresh cranberries
225g/8oz caster sugar
11g/½oz sachet powdered
  gelatine
125ml/4fl oz fresh orange juice
100g/4oz celery, chopped
100g/4oz apple, peeled and
  chopped
100g/4oz walnuts, chopped
Lettuce leaves to garnish
Mayonnaise, soured or whipped
  cream to serve

1   Wash the cranberries, drain and remove any stems. Using a blender or food processor blend the cranberries thoroughly. Add the sugar and leave for 15 minutes, stirring occasionally. In a small saucepan sprinkle the gelatine over the orange juice and allow to dissolve over a very low heat.

2   Add the gelatine mixture to the cranberries with the celery, apple and nuts and mix well. Put the mixture into a mould and chill thoroughly in the refrigerator for 6—8 hours.

Serving suggestion: Turn out on to a serving dish lined with lettuce leaves and serve with mayonnaise, soured or whipped cream.

Pigeon Casserole
with Juniper Berries

Serves 4   Preparation time: 20 minutes   Cooking time: 2—2½ hours

100ml/4fl oz vegetable oil
4 oven-ready pigeons
75g/3oz bacon, rind removed
  and chopped
1 carrot, peeled and chopped
1 onion, peeled and chopped
4 tablespoons flour
4 tablespoons tomato purée
425ml/¾ pint stock
2 bay-leaves
1 bouquet garni
Salt and freshly ground black
  pepper
9 juniper berries, crushed
1 clove garlic, crushed

Pre-heat the oven to 170°C/325°F/Gas Mark 3.

1   In a large frying pan, heat the oil and brown the pigeons all over. Remove
    to a large casserole and fry the bacon, carrot and onion in the remaining
    oil. Place in the casserole with the pigeons. Add the flour and tomato purée
    to the frying pan and stir over the heat for 2 minutes.

2   Add the stock, herbs, salt and pepper to taste. Add the crushed berries and
    garlic and boil the mixture for a further 2 minutes. Pour over the pigeons
    and cook them in the oven for 2—2½ hours.

Serving suggestion: Serve with boiled rice and freshly cooked vegetables.

Mackerel with Lemon Gooseberry Sauce

Serves 4   Preparation time: 30 minutes   Cooking time: 10 minutes

'Come all ye jovial gardeners, and listen unto me,
Whilst I relate the different sorts of winning gooseberries.
This famous institution was founded long ago,
That men might meet, and drink, and have a gooseberry show.'

From 'The Gooseberry Grower's Song', 1885

For the mackerel:
4 mackerel, cleaned
1 onion, chopped
1 carrot, chopped
1 bay-leaf
Salt and freshly ground pepper

For the sauce:
25g/1oz butter
25g/1oz flour
225g/8oz gooseberries, cooked
  and puréed
1 tablespoon chopped chives
Juice of 1 lemon

1   In a saucepan, cover the mackerel with water and add the onion, carrot, bay-leaf and seasoning. Bring to the boil and simmer for 10 minutes until the fish is tender. Remove the fish and reserve the liquid.

2   To make the sauce, melt the butter in another saucepan and add the flour, mixing well over the heat. Slowly add 150ml/¼ pint of the reserved fish liquid, stirring constantly, and then add the puréed gooseberries. Bring to the boil, stirring. Add the chives and the lemon juice and cook for 5 minutes.

Serving suggestion: Serve the sauce with the mackerel.

CHAPTER 4

PERFECTLY PLUM

As far back as the sixteenth century, Little Jack Horner 'stuck in his thumb' and immortalised the plum in one of the world's best known nursery rhymes. Of course, he did not have the selection to choose from that we do today, but nevertheless, the plum had been a favourite for centuries. Today, thanks to the abundance of pick-your-own sites and farm-shops around the country, we are encouraged to discover the many different varieties now available.

Perhaps the best known and most popular plum, ideal for cooking, preserving and eating, is the Victoria, which first appeared in 1840. The Pershore Yellow Egg, which received its name from its place of origin and rather distinct colour, is also especially good for cooking and jam-making. This variety has a long history and has played a significant part in developing many new varieties that we see on the shelves today. Other good cooking varieties are the small, dark purple Czar, named after a visiting Russian emperor over 100 years ago; the Pershore Purple Egg, available in late August; the golden Warwickshire Drooper; the autumn Monarch and Marjories Seedling, and the excellent jam-making Wyedale.

Although all plums can be cooked, it is best to stick to these culinary types as they are less expensive and have a lower sugar content. Buy your plums ripe but firm. It may be necessary to keep them for a few days to ripen properly.

I have also included some recipes using prunes. Most of the prunes we use are imported but as they are wonderfully versatile for all manner of cooking, we can perhaps learn to appreciate just how valuable they are.

Plum Ring with Apricot Sauce

Serves 6   Preparation time: 20 minutes   Setting time: 5 hours

You could actually reverse this lovely dish by making it an apricot ring with plum sauce. Either way it is a wonderful combination of flavours.

For the plum ring:
450g/1lb plums, stoned and
  halved
2 tablespoons sugar
3 teaspoons powdered gelatine
275ml/½ pint whipping cream
2 egg whites
1 tablespoon sherry
Slices of plum to garnish

For the apricot sauce:
450ml/16fl oz water
100g/4oz sugar
1 teaspoon vanilla essence
3 teaspoons lemon juice
350g/12oz apricots, stoned and
  halved
2 tablespoons icing sugar

1   In a saucepan place the plums with 3 tablespoons water and cook for 5 minutes, until they are tender. Using a blender or food processor, purée the plums and add the sugar. Place the gelatine in a small bowl with 3 tablespoons of water and place over a pan of hot water to allow the gelatine to dissolve. Stir in the plum mixture and leave in the refrigerator until almost set. Whip the cream until soft and fold into the plum mixture. Whip the egg whites until stiff and fold in with the sherry. Pour into a ring mould and place in the refrigerator to set.

2   For the apricot sauce, make the syrup by putting the water, sugar and vanilla into a saucepan and stirring over the heat until dissolved. Bring to the boil, add the lemon juice and the apricots and poach for 6 minutes.

3   In a blender or food processor, purée the mixture with the icing sugar until smooth.

Serving suggestion: Unmould the plum ring on to a serving dish and garnish with plum slices. Pour some of the sauce over the plum ring and serve the remaining separately.

Fresh Fruit Salad
with Creamy Plum Sauce

Serves 4—6   Preparation time: 20 minutes   Chilling time: 1 hour

Here is just a guideline for a fresh fruit salad, but you can, of course, adjust it to suit your tastes and the fruits available. It really is the plum sauce that makes this a special dish.

For the salad:
2 apples, cored and sliced
2 oranges, peeled and segmented
50g/2oz green seedless grapes
50g/2oz black seedless grapes
100g/4oz raspberries, hulled
100/4oz strawberries, hulled
2 bananas, peeled and sliced
100g/4oz cherries, stoned
2 kiwi fruit, peeled and sliced
Juice of ½ lemon
75g/3oz sugar

For the sauce:
4 plums, stoned and halved
100g/4oz icing sugar
225g/8oz cream cheese
1 tablespoon lemon juice

---

1   Mix all the prepared fruit together in a bowl. Sprinkle with the lemon juice and sugar, toss well and chill in the refrigerator for 1 hour.

---

2   Meanwhile make the sauce. Using a blender or food processor, blend together the plums and sugar until smooth. Add the cream cheese and lemon juice and beat well. Cover and chill until ready to serve.

Serving suggestion: Divide the fruit salad between individual bowls and serve topped with the sauce.

Deep-dish Plum Pie

Serves 6—8   Preparation time: 1 hour 20 minutes   Cooking time: 1 hour

For the filling:
1.8kg/4lb slightly under ripe
  plums, stoned and sliced into
  eighths
275g/10oz sugar
50g/2oz flour
Finely grated rind of 1 orange

For the pastry:
225g/8oz plain flour
Pinch of salt
100g/4oz unsalted butter, chilled
50g/2oz icing sugar, sifted
2 egg yolks
2 tablespoons cold water
Beaten egg to glaze

Pre-heat the oven to 190°C/375°F/Gas Mark 5.

---

1   In a bowl mix together the plums, sugar, flour and the grated orange rind. Leave to stand for 30 minutes, stirring occasionally.

---

2   To make the pastry, sift the flour and salt into a bowl. Chop in the cold butter and rub in until the mixture resembles fine breadcrumbs. Add the icing sugar and mix in well. Mix together the egg yolks and water and add to the flour mixture. Using a fork, combine to a firm dough, cover and chill thoroughly in the refrigerator.

---

3   Lightly butter a 1.1 litre/2 pint baking dish and pour in the plum mixture. Bake for 25 minutes until bubbling. Roll out the pastry to 5mm/¼in thick and, using a 6.5cm/2½in round biscuit cutter, cut out rounds. Arrange over the hot plums, overlapping slightly and leaving a 1cm/½in gap around the edge. Brush with beaten egg and bake for 30—35 minutes until golden brown.

Serving suggestion: Serve warm with whipped cream or vanilla ice-cream.

Cold Plum Soup

Serves 4   Preparation time: 15 minutes   Cooking time: 15 minutes

This unusual starter is ideal for a summer dinner party.

225ml/8fl oz apple juice
175ml/6fl oz dry white wine
Pinch each cinnamon, ginger
  and cloves
350g/¾lb fresh dark plums
100g/4fl oz single cream
1 tablespoon lemon juice

1   In a saucepan put the apple juice, 100ml/4fl oz of the wine and the spices. Bring to the boil. Stone and chop the plums, add to the saucepan and continue simmering for 15 minutes until the plums are very soft. Strain into a bowl and add the sugar, adjusting to taste. Chill thoroughly.

2   In a blender or food processor blend the remaining wine, cream and lemon juice.

Serving suggestion: Serve the soup chilled with a swirl of the lemon cream.

Peking Duck with Plum Sauce

Serves 5—10   Preparation time: see below   Cooking time: see below

This dish is very popular with guests and is great fun to eat. It is ideal as a starter, main course, or part of a big Chinese feast.

For the duckling:
1 × 1.75—2.75kg/4—6lb duckling
3 tablespoons honey
1 tablespoon dry sherry
2 tablespoons water
Very thinly sliced cucumbers and
  spring onions to serve

For the pancakes:
175g/6oz plain flour
150ml/¼ pint boiling water
3 tablespoons sesame oil

For the plum sauce:
12 fresh dark plums
6 tablespoons water
3 tablespoons soy jam
1 tablespoon sugar

1   The sauce can be made in advance if stored in the refrigerator. Peel, stone and cut the plums into quarters. Place in a saucepan with the water and simmer gently until the plums are very soft. Add the soy jam and sugar and continue cooking for 10—12 minutes, stirring constantly. Pour the sauce into jars and, when cool, cover and keep in the refrigerator until ready to use.

2   To make the pancakes, sift the flour into a bowl and very gradually add the boiling water, beating into a firm dough. Knead for about 4 minutes, cover the bowl with a linen towel and allow to stand for about 10 minutes. Roll the dough into a long sausage shape, about 5cm/2in in diameter, and cut into 20 slices of 1cm/½in thickness. Brush each slice on one side with sesame oil and sandwich in twos, oiled sides together.

3 Take a heavy frying pan, ungreased, and heat to very hot. Place the double-sided pancakes in the pan and cook for about 2 minutes on each side and until brown spots have appeared. Remove, pull the two sides apart and fold each in a semi-circle, greased side inside. Stack on a plate and keep warm. Before serving, place in a steamer and steam for about 10 minutes.

Pre-heat the oven to 200°C/400°F/Gas Mark 5.

4 Place the duck in a saucepan, cover with boiling water and boil for 3-5 minutes. Remove from the pan, rinse under cold water and pat dry with kitchen paper. Combine the honey, sherry and water and brush all over the duck. Place on a rack in a roasting pan and bake for 30 minutes, then reduce the heat to 190°C/375°F/Gas Mark 5, and cook for a further 40 minutes.

5 To prepare the duck, first slice the crisp skin and remove any fat. Arrange the skin on a serving dish with sliced meat. Serve the wings and drumsticks separately. Now for the true magic...

Serving suggestion: Each guest should take a pancake and spread with plum sauce. Place a slice of duck on top with slices of cucumber and spring onion. Roll up the pancake and tuck in.

Note: Soy jam can be obtained from any Chinese supermarket or other specialist shop.

Veal with Oranges and Plums

Serves 4   Preparation time: 1 hour   Cooking time: 1½ hours

4 veal chops, 5cm/2in thick
Salt and freshly ground black pepper
25g/1oz plain flour
2 tablespoons butter
2 tablespoons oil
1 onion, very finely chopped
1 carrot, very finely chopped
1 large orange
1 teaspoon dried thyme
2 parsley sprigs
1 bay-leaf
125ml/4fl oz red wine
2 cloves garlic, crushed
350ml/12fl oz rich stock
100g/4oz pickling onions
16 plums, stoned and halved
1 tablespoon freshly chopped parsley

Pre-heat the oven to 180°C/350°F/Gas Mark 4.

1   Pat the veal dry with kitchen paper, sprinkle with salt and pepper and dredge in the flour. Melt the butter and oil in a heavy frying pan and cook the veal on both sides until brown. Transfer to a plate.

2   Reduce the heat and add the onion and carrot, stirring until the vegetables are tender. Cut a large strip of peel from the orange and tie in a piece of cheesecloth along with the thyme, parsley and bay-leaf. Add to the pan with the wine and garlic. Boil, stirring continuously until the liquid almost evaporates. Add the veal and stock and return to the boil. Transfer to a baking dish, cover and bake in the oven until the veal is very tender (1½ hours).

3   While the meat is cooking, parboil the onions and drain. From half the orange, cut the rind into very fine julienne. Cut the whole orange into segments, removing all the white pith.

4 Remove the herb bag from the veal. Transfer the veal to a plate and keep warm. Strain the cooking liquid and discard the vegetables. Return the liquid to the pan and add the plums and onions. Bring to the boil and simmer until the onions are just tender. Using a perforated spoon remove the plums and onions and arrange around the veal. Boil the liquid until reduced to 175ml/ 6fl oz and add the orange julienne. Simmer for 1 minute then adjust the seasoning.

Serving suggestion: Spoon the sauce over the veal, garnished with the orange segments, and sprinkle with the freshly chopped parsley.

Braised Pork Chops with Plums

Serves 4   Preparation time: 20 minutes   Cooking time: 1 hour

This recipe can also be made using canned plums, in which case use the syrup from the can.

350g/12oz plums, stoned
5 tablespoons sugar
3 tablespoons cider vinegar
50ml/2fl oz water
1 tablespoon butter
4 pork chops, trimmed
Salt and freshly ground black
    pepper
1 tablespoon flour blended with
    4 tablespoons water

1   First put the plums, sugar, vinegar and water in a saucepan. Heat and simmer until the plums are soft and the liquid syrupy. Remove the plums with a perforated spoon and put to one side.

2   Melt the butter in a frying pan and add the pork chops, browning well on both sides. Season with salt and pepper. Make up the quantity of plum syrup to 175ml/6fl oz with water and add to the chops. Simmer for 45 minutes.

3   Skim off any fat and add the flour blended with water to thicken the sauce. Add the plums and simmer gently for a further 5 minutes.

Serving suggestion: Serve immediately with plenty of fresh vegetables and creamy mashed potatoes.

Fruit Beef Stew

Serves 6   Preparation time: 30 minutes   Cooking time: 3 hours 25 minutes

225g/8oz bacon, chopped
1.1kg/3lb stewing beef, cut into
  5cm/2in pieces
Flour to dust
Salt and freshly ground black
  pepper
3 onions, finely sliced
3 cloves garlic, crushed
5 tablespoons tomato purée
1½ teaspoons paprika
350ml/12fl oz dark beer
225ml/8fl oz beef stock
50ml/2fl oz brandy
225g/8oz plums, stoned
100g/4oz dried apricots
2 sprigs thyme
1 bay-leaf
2 tablespoons lemon juice
1 tablespoon grated lemon rind
Fresh parsley to garnish

---

1   First blanch the chopped bacon in boiling water for about 5 minutes. Drain and put aside.

---

2   Dust the beef with the flour. Heat the oil in a large casserole and fry the beef in batches for 10 minutes, turning until brown and crisp. Season with salt and pepper, remove from the casserole with a perforated spoon and put aside. Add the bacon and onions to the casserole and cook until soft. Add the garlic and cook for 5 minutes, stirring. Then add the tomato purée and paprika. Add the beer, stock and brandy and boil until the mixture is reduced by half. Add the beef, fruit, thyme and bay-leaf. Simmer, half covered, for about 2½ hours.

---

3   Add the lemon juice and rind and season. Cook for a further 15 minutes uncovered.

Serving suggestion: Serve garnished with fresh parsley on a bed of hot buttered noodles.

Glazed Ham with Plum Sauce

Serves 6—8   Preparation time: 10 minutes   Cooking time: 3 hours

This plum sauce is made using canned red plums and goes especially well with ham, duck or game.

For the ham:
1.8kg/4lb middle gammon joint
2 bay-leaves
1 onion, peeled (and studded
  with cloves if liked)
575ml/1 pint dry cider

For the glaze:
3 tablespoons runny honey
2 tablespoons brown sugar
1 teaspoon cinnamon

For the plum sauce:
570g/20oz tin red plums in syrup
2 tablespoons vinegar
2 tablespoons sugar
Pinch of allspice

---

1   First prepare the gammon. Place the joint in a large saucepan, cover with water and bring to the boil. Remove from the heat and discard the water. Place the joint back in the saucepan, add the bay-leaves, onion, cider and enough water to cover. Bring to the boil, cover and cook gently for 2 hours.

---

2   Meanwhile make the plum sauce. Place all the sauce ingredients in a saucepan and simmer for about 15 minutes. Press the mixture through a fine sieve, return to the saucepan and re-heat.

Pre-heat the oven to 190°C/375°F/Gas Mark 5.

3 When the ham is cooked, remove from the cooking juices, place on a roasting tin and reserve the juices. In a small pan heat together the honey, sugar and cinnamon until they develop a thin consistency. With a sharp knife score the fat on the ham in a diamond pattern and baste with the honey mixture. Pour in some of the reserved juices and bake for about 30 minutes, basting occasionally until the ham is crisp and golden.

Serving suggestion: Serve the ham with the plum sauce, either hot or cold, with lots of fresh vegetables.

Port and Plum Sorbet

Serves 4—6   Preparation time: 30 minutes   Freezing time: 2 hours

A refreshing way to end any meal.

225ml/8fl oz port
225ml/8fl oz water
75g/3oz sugar
450g/1lb plums, stoned and chopped
2 tablespoons lemon juice

1   In a large saucepan heat together the port, water and sugar, stirring until the sugar has dissolved. Simmer for 5 minutes, then leave to cool. Using a blender or food processor, purée the plums, then pass them through a fine sieve into a bowl, removing all skin. Add the port syrup and lemon juice, cover and chill thoroughly.

2   Pour the mixture into an ice-making tray and freeze until solid, stirring the mixture occasionally to prevent crystallisation. Cover and leave in the freezer for at least 2 hours before serving to improve the flavours.

Serving suggestion: Allow to soften slightly before serving.

Top left Apple and Blackberry Crunch (page 26)
Top right Lil's Apple Cake (page 28).
Left Chicken Fruit Salad (page 29) **Right** Pear Bisque (page 38)

Top   *Rhubarb Shortbread Layer (page 49)*
Left   *Indian Fruit Rice with Pine Nuts (page 51)*
Right   *Duck and Cherry Mousse (page 55)*
Bottom   *Orange and Rhubarb Compote (page 43)*

Top left *Cranberry Bread (page 79)*
Top right *Strawberry and Raspberry Soufflé (page 62)*
Left *Mackerel with Lemon Gooseberry Sauce (page 82)*
Right *Dipped Strawberries with Soured Cream (page 66)*

Top Raspberry Salad (page 69) **Left** Little Berry Pizzas (page 67)
Right Blackberry Fool (page 70)
Bottom Pigeon Casserole with Juniper Berries (page 81)

Devils on Horseback

Makes 12   Preparation time: 1 hour   Cooking time: 15 minutes

These little devils are ideal party appetisers!

12 prunes
12 rashers sweet-cured bacon
3 slices fried bread

Microwave: Prepare as directed and place on a roasting rack or on kitchen paper. Cook on power 7 for 5—6 minutes until crisp.

---

1   To soften the prunes, first soak them in plain unsweetened tea for 1 hour. Remove the stones, pat the prunes dry with kitchen paper and wrap each one in a rasher of bacon. Secure with a wooden cocktail stick and place on a sheet of foil.

---

2   Place the devils under a hot grill and cook until crisp, turning occasionally. Cut each piece of fried bread into 4 triangles and serve topped with a warm devil.

Serving suggestion: Serve immediately.

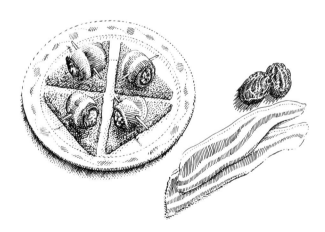

Prune Bread

Makes 1 loaf   Preparation time: 30 minutes   Baking time: 1 hour

A lovely treat for all the family!

225g/8oz prunes, stoned
225g/8oz plain flour
150g/5oz sugar
1 teaspoon bicarbonate of soda
½ teaspoon salt
1 egg
2 tablespoons melted butter

Pre-heat the oven to 180°C/350°F/Gas Mark 4.

1   In a saucepan place the prunes with 350ml/12fl oz water. Bring to the boil and simmer for 10 minutes. Grease a 450g/1lb loaf tin. In a bowl sift the flour, sugar, soda and salt.

2   Drain the prunes reserving the liquid. Chop the prunes, add to the reserved liquid and make up the quantity, if necessary, to 450ml/16fl oz with water. Cream together the egg and melted butter. Add the prune mixture and blend well. Add the flour mixture and mix until smooth.

3   Turn into the prepared loaf tin and bake for 50—60 minutes or until a cake tester inserted comes out clean. Leave to cool slightly before turning out on to a wire rack. Wrap in foil and leave in the refrigerator overnight before serving.

Serving suggestion: Serve with butter on its own for a delicious taste.

Freezing: This loaf freezes extremely well. Wrap well in foil and secure in a plastic bag. It will keep for up to 3 months.

Creamy Prune Tart

Serves 8—10   Preparation time: 30 minutes   Cooking time: 25 minutes

For the pastry:
225g/8oz plain flour
Pinch of salt
100g/4oz butter
4 tablespoons cold water

For the prune cream:
225g/8oz stoned prunes
  (vacuum-packed)
2 tablespoons water
2 tablespoons brandy
2 tablespoons sugar
3 tablespoons double or whipping
  cream

Pre-heat the oven to 190°C/375°F/Gas Mark 5.

1   Make the pastry by combining the flour and salt in a bowl. Rub in the butter until the mixture resembles fine breadcrumbs. Add enough water to form a stiff dough, mixing in with a fork. Leave aside for 20 minutes.

2   Roll out the pastry on a lightly floured surface to 2.5mm/⅛in thick and place into a 25cm/10in flan tin with a removable bottom. Press into the bottom and sides and trim the edges. Pierce the base with a fork, line with foil and fill with pastry weights. Bake blind for 10 minutes and then remove the foil and weights and bake for a further 15 minutes. Leave to cool.

3   Place the prunes in a bowl and cover with boiling water. Leave for 5 minutes and drain. Place the prunes, 2 tablespoons water, brandy and sugar in a blender or food processor and purée. Spread the mixture into the prepared crust.

Serving suggestion: Drizzle the cream over the top.

Peppers Stuffed
with Prune Cream Cheese

Serves 6   Preparation time: 20 minutes   Chilling time: 1—2 hours

1 green pepper
1 red pepper
1 yellow pepper
3 × 75g/3oz packets of cream
  cheese
Juice of ½ lemon
Rind of 1 lemon, finely grated
20 soaked prunes, stoned and
  finely chopped
Freshly ground black pepper

1   Wash the peppers, cut off the tops and scoop out all the seeds and white
    pith. Dry inside and outside with kitchen paper. In a bowl, cream the cream
    cheese with the lemon juice and rind. Add the chopped prunes and season
    with black pepper.

2   Stuff each pepper with the mixture and press well into the cavity with the
    back of a spoon. Cover with cling-film and chill thoroughly in the refrigerator.

Serving suggestion: To serve, thinly slice the peppers into 5mm/¼in thick rings
and arrange the different colours on individual plates. Serve with buttered bread
triangles.

Prunes with Noodles

Serves 6—8   Cooking time: 1 hour

This unusual combination is a traditional Good Friday dish served in several countries around Europe.

450g/1lb prunes, stoned
50g/2oz sugar
½ lemon, thinly sliced
1 stick cinnamon
6 slices bread, crusts removed
50g/2oz butter
225g/8oz noodles

Microwave: To cook the noodles in the microwave, place them in a dish with 500ml/1 pint of water and 1 teaspoon salt. You may also add 1 tablespoon of oil if you like. Cook on high power for 6 minutes. Allow to stand for 3 minutes before serving.

1   First prepare the prunes. Place them in a saucepan and just cover with water. Bring to the boil and simmer gently for about 20 minutes. Add the sugar, sliced lemon and cinnamon stick and continue cooking for 10 minutes. Set aside.

2   Cut the bread slices into cubes. Melt all but 1 tablespoon of the butter in a frying pan and fry the bread cubes until crisp and brown on both sides. Keep warm. Cook the noodles in a saucepan of boiling water and a little salt until soft (8—10 minutes). Drain and toss with the remaining butter.

Serving suggestion: To serve put the hot noodles in a serving dish and scatter the hot *croûtons* over the top. Serve the prunes in a separate bowl.

Pork and Prune Stew

Serves 6   Preparation time: 20 minutes   Cooking time: 2 hours

2 onions
1.1kg/3lb boneless pork shoulder,
  cut into 3cm/1½in cubes
50ml/2fl oz fresh orange juice
50ml/2fl oz soy sauce
25ml/1fl oz sherry
1½ tablespoons freshly chopped
  ginger
1 tablespoon cornflour dissolved
  in 1 tablespoon water
225g/8oz prunes, stoned

Pre-heat the oven to 170°C/325°F/Gas Mark 3.

1   Place the whole, unpeeled onions in the centre of a Swiss roll tin. Distribute the pork around the tin in a single layer and bake for 1 hour, turning the pork occasionally.

2   Cool the onions slightly, peel, quarter and place in a baking tray. Add the pork, orange juice, soy sauce, sherry and ginger and continue to bake for a further 1 hour until the pork is tender. Remove the pork with a perforated spoon and pour the juices into a large saucepan.

3   Place the saucepan over the heat and add the dissolved cornflour. Bring to the boil and boil for about 3 minutes, stirring until the mixture thickens. Add the pork, onions and prunes and cook until heated through.

Serving suggestion: Serve with rice or buttered noodles.

Pork and Prune Casserole

Serves 4   Preparation time: 10 minutes   Cooking time: 1¼ hours

450g/1lb pork fillet, trimmed and
  cut into cubes
225g/8oz dried prunes, stoned
2 cooking apples, peeled, cored
  and sliced
1 onion, sliced
3 potatoes, diced
Salt and freshly ground black
  pepper
4 tablespoons fresh sage,
  chopped
275ml/½ pint dry cider
Fresh sage to garnish

Pre-heat the oven to 190°C/375°F/Gas Mark 5.
Microwave: Prepare as described but use only 150ml/¼ pint cider. Cover and
cook on high power for 5 minutes. Stir and then cook for a further 25—30 minutes
on medium power or until the pork is tender. Stir once during cooking and add
more cider if necessary. Allow to stand for 5 minutes before serving.

1   In a large casserole place the pork, prunes, apples, onion, potatoes and season-
    ing. Sprinkle over the fresh sage and add the cider.

2   Cover and cook for 1¼ hours or until the pork is tender.

Serving suggestion: Garnish with fresh sage and serve with creamy mashed
potatoes and fresh vegetables.

Fresh Fruit Salad Dip

Serves 8   Preparation time: 30 minutes

This fruit salad has a rather unusual dressing and is perfect for a buffet table.
Use any fruits you wish.

For the salad:
2 large seedless oranges
2 large bananas
2 firm pears
2 apples
225g/8oz seedless grapes
450g/1lb sweet plums
75g/3oz dates, stoned and halved

For the dressing:
225ml/8fl oz soured cream
3 tablespoons maple syrup
Pinch of salt

---

1   First make the dressing by combining the three ingredients in a bowl. Cover
    and refrigerate until ready to use.

---

2   Peel the oranges and split into segments. Cut the bananas into bite-sized pieces.
    Cut the pears and apples into bite-sized wedges. Wash the grapes and separate
    into clusters. Slice the plums into quarters. Spoon the dressing into a bowl
    in the middle of a round platter. Arrange the fruit attractively around the
    dressing and garnish with the date halves.

Serving suggestion: Serve with wooden cocktail sticks to dip each piece of fruit
into the dressing.

CHAPTER 5

AN ABUNDANCE OF CURRANTS

Red, black and white currants have been grown in the gardens of Britain since early in the sixteenth century. Once mistakenly believed to be the fruit from which the raisin of Corinth was derived, it is from this fruit, dried and used in cakes and other baking, that the name currant originated.

Today, the less sharp white variety is virtually unobtainable in shops and is only grown by few private gardeners and nurseries. The red currant, with its rather distinctive sweet-sour taste is not only one of the most delicious of British fruits but also one of the most beautiful and versatile. Sprigs of plump, juicy, glistening red berries may be eaten raw, but are especially delicious cooked in pies, puddings and tarts, or simply poached with a little sugar. Both red and black currants are excellent for making sauces, syrups and flavouring jellies. Because black currants are particularly rich in vitamin C, they have long been regarded as a very important medicinal fruit. Once known as the quinsy berry, the black currant is still renowned today for its soothing properties in treating coughs and colds.

When buying currants, look for firm, clean, glossy bunches, avoiding anything dusty looking, and check that there are not many leaves or empty stalks included. They will keep very well for up to 10 days if covered in the refrigerator.

You will find in this chapter a host of exciting recipes using red and black currants in savoury and sweet dishes, but remember that you may use either fruit in most cases, depending on your preference and what is available.

Game Pie

Serves 6   Preparation time: 1 hour   Cooking time: 1 hour 20 minutes

A traditional cold raised pie of game and other meats, encased in a thick shell of hot-water crust pastry, is a lovely starter to a meal and also a super addition to a summer picnic.

For the filling:
350g/12oz sausage-meat
100g/4oz cooked ham, cubed
175g/6oz cooked beef chuck
  steak, cubed
1 cooked pheasant, meat cut into
  small pieces
100g/4oz red currants, topped
  and tailed
Salt and freshly ground pepper
275ml/½ pint brown stock

For the pastry:
350g/12oz plain flour
1½ teaspoons salt
75g/3oz lard
150ml/¼ pint milk
Beaten egg to glaze

---

1   Make the pastry by mixing the flour and salt. Melt the lard in the milk, bring to the boil and add to the dry ingredients. Beat together very quickly to a soft dough. Knead until smooth. Cover with cling-film and leave for 20—30 minutes.

Pre-heat the oven to 220°C/425°F/Gas Mark 7.

---

2   Cut off three-quarters of the pastry and roll out into an oval shape about 5mm/¼in thick. Place an 18cm/7in hinged pie mould on to a baking sheet and carefully lift the rolled out pastry on to it. Press carefully into the mould and leave about 5mm/¼in pastry standing above the rim.

3   Press the sausage meat over the bottom and sides of the pastry using the back of the spoon. In a bowl mix together the ham, steak, game and currants and season well. Pack firmly into the pie and pour over the stock. Roll out the remaining pastry and place over the top. Dampen the edges and pinch together. Cut a hole in the centre of the lid. Bake for 20 minutes and then reduce the heat to 180°C/350°F/Gas Mark 4. Cook for 1 hour or until the meat is tender when tested with a skewer. Remove the sides of the tin and brush all over with beaten egg. Return to the oven for 30 minutes to finish cooking.

Serving suggestion: Serve with crusty bread and lashings of pickle for a traditional country lunch.

Lamb En Croute

Serves 4   Preparation time: 30 minutes   Cooking time: 35—40 minutes

For the lamb:
4 lamb chump chops, 1cm/½in
  thick
375g/13oz packet frozen puff
  pastry, thawed
Salt and freshly ground pepper
1 teaspoon freshly chopped
  rosemary
50g/2oz chicken liver paté
Beaten egg to glaze
Sprigs of fresh rosemary to serve

For the sauce:
50g/2oz butter
225g/8oz red currants, topped
  and tailed
450g/1lb sweet apples, peeled,
  cored and sliced
1 teaspoon sugar

Pre-heat the oven to 220°C/425°F/Gas Mark 7.

---

1   First trim the lamb chops of any excess fat. Roll out the pastry and divide
    into 4 portions large enough to wrap around each chop. Place a chop on each
    pastry portion, season and sprinkle with the chopped rosemary. Spread each
    with the liver pâté, wrap around the pastry and seal the edges. Decorate with
    any remaining pastry and brush with beaten egg. Place on a baking tray and
    bake for 35—40 minutes until golden brown.

---

2   Meanwhile, make the red currant and apple sauce. In a saucepan, melt the
    butter, add the fruit and cover and cook gently until the fruit is very soft.
    Stir in the sugar then pass through a fine sieve.

Serving suggestion: Pour the sauce on to individual plates and place the lamb
chops on top. Decorate with a sprig of fresh rosemary and serve with a crisp salad
or fresh vegetables.

Roast Pheasant
with Red Currant Jelly Sauce

Serves 3—4   Preparation time: 25 minutes   Cooking time: 40 minutes

When choosing a pheasant, make sure it has been hung to your liking before cooking. The cock bird is generally larger than the hen but the hen has more flesh and is usually juicier. Younger birds are best of all. A good pheasant will feed 3—4 people.

For the pheasant:
1 pheasant
3 rashers streaky bacon
Salt and freshly ground pepper
Butter for basting
Flour for dusting

For the sauce:
1 stick cinnamon
12 cloves
50g/2oz sugar
Grated rind of 1 lemon
175ml/6fl oz red wine
225g/8oz red currant jelly
(see page 112)

Pre-heat the oven to 200°C/400°F/Gas Mark 6.
Microwave: To cook the pheasant in the microwave, follow the instructions for cooking duck on page 54, still covering the breast with the bacon. Cook on power 7 for 7 minutes per 450g/1lb weight. Allow to stand for 3 minutes after cooking.

1   Cover the breast of the pheasant with the rashers of bacon and season with salt and pepper. Place in a roasting tin, baste with the melted butter and roast for about 40 minutes, depending on size. Baste once during cooking. 10 minutes before the end of cooking, remove the bacon and dust with a little flour. Return to the oven to brown.

2   To make the sauce, first crush the cinnamon and cloves into a small saucepan and add the sugar, lemon rind and wine. Simmer gently for 10 minutes, then strain. Add the jelly to the strained liquid and stir until the jelly has dissolved. Simmer the mixture for a further 5 minutes.

Serving suggestion: Serve the pheasant with plenty of the red currant jelly sauce, either warm or cold.

Roast Venison with Currant Sauce

Serves 6—8   Preparation time: see below   Cooking time: 1 hour 45 minutes

For the venison:
1 × 1.5kg/4lb loin of venison
5 peppercorns
Fresh parsley sprigs
1 bay-leaf
2 carrots, chopped
2 onions, chopped
1 stick celery, chopped
Red wine (see below)
4 tablespoons vegetable oil
3 tablespoons flour

For the sauce:
275ml/½ pint port
15g/½oz breadcrumbs
100g/4oz sugar
2 tablespoons butter
½ teaspoon cinnamon
½ teaspoon ground cloves
50g/2oz red or black currants,
  trimmed

Pre-heat the oven to 170°C/325°F/Gas Mark 3.

1 Place the venison with the peppercorns, parsley, bay-leaf, vegetables and enough red wine to half cover and leave to marinate for about 12 hours, turning occasionally.

2 Make the sauce by combining all the sauce ingredients except the currants in a saucepan and bringing to the boil. Simmer until the mixture is thickened and syrupy. Add the currants, adjust the seasoning and continue cooking until the currants are soft (10 minutes).

3 Place the meat in a roasting tin and brush with the oil. Reserve the marinade. Cover with foil and roast for 1 hour 25 minutes. Remove the foil and dust the joint with 2 tablespoons of the flour. Return to the oven and roast for a further 20 minutes. Keep warm. Pour the marinade into a saucepan and boil until the quantity is reduced by half. Skim off the fat in the roasting tin and add the remaining flour, stirring over the heat. Stir in the marinade and boil for 2 minutes. Strain.

Serving suggestion: Serve the venison with the tasty gravy and the currant sauce.

Roast Stuffed Partridges

Serves 4   Preparation time: 45 minutes   Cooking time: 50—60 minutes

Partridges are small birds and usually one is served per person. However, you may find that with this stuffing, half each is sufficient.

For the stuffing:
50g/2oz butter or margarine
40g/1½oz finely chopped onion
40g/1½oz finely chopped celery
50g/2oz chopped walnuts
75g/3oz fresh red currants,
  topped and tailed
40g/1½oz sugar
50ml/2fl oz orange juice
1 tablespoon grated orange rind
1 small sliced loaf, wholewheat
  or raisin bread, toasted
Salt and freshly ground black
  pepper
Sprinkle dried savory
½ teaspoon poultry seasoning

For the partridges:
4 partridges
25g/1oz butter
8 rashers streaky bacon, rind
  removed
Watercress and potato
  crisps to garnish

Pre-heat the oven to 220°C/425°F/Gas Mark 7.

1   Make the stuffing first. In a frying pan melt the butter or margarine and sauté the onion, celery and nuts for 5 minutes. Add the red currants, sugar, orange juice and rind and continue cooking, stirring constantly until the red currants soften. Put aside for 20 minutes.

2   Cut the toasted bread slices into 1cm/½in cubes and place in a bowl with the salt and pepper, savory and poultry seasoning. Mix well and add the currant mixture. Combine thoroughly and use to stuff each partridge.

3   Spread the butter over each bird and place one rasher of bacon over each breast. Bake for 50—60 minutes until cooked.

Serving suggestion: Garnish with watercress and potato crisps and serve with a light salad.

Red Currant Jelly

Makes 1.1kg/3lb   Preparation time: 10 minutes   Cooking time: 45 minutes

This brightly-coloured jelly is a valuable addition to any larder. As well as a good accompaniment to meats such as lamb, venison and pheasant, it can be used as a fruit glaze. You can, of course, also make this jelly using black currants.

1.1kg/3lb red currants, trimmed
575ml/1 pint water
Sugar (see below)

1   Place the fruit and water in a saucepan and cook for 30 minutes until the fruit is really tender. Press through a fine sieve or muslin cloth into another saucepan. For every 575ml/1 pint of liquid add 350ml/12oz of sugar.

2   Dissolve the sugar into the mixture over a low heat and then bring to the boil, boiling rapidly until the mixture reaches a temperature of 105°C/221°F (setting point) or a teaspoonful of the mixture wrinkles when dropped on to a cold plate and pushed with a finger.

3   Pour into clean, warmed jam jars and cover with a wax disc, wax side down. Top with a screw lid and label with name and date.

Serving suggestion: This jelly can be served with any hot or cold meats, particularly lamb, venison or pheasant.

Variation: To use this jelly as a fruit glaze, simply heat the required amount over the medium heat until smooth and brush or spoon over the fruit. You may like to add a touch of extra flavouring, such as kirsch, for an extra special glaze.

Healthy Fruit Salad

Serves 4   Preparation time: 20 minutes

This salad is packed with goodness. You can use any of your favourite fruits.

For the salad:
1 iceberg lettuce
1 small melon in season
1 grapefruit
1 orange
100g/4oz black, seedless grapes
100g/4oz strawberries, halved
100g/4oz raspberries, hulled
100g/4oz wheatgerm, toasted
4 sprigs red currants, washed,
  to serve

For the dressing:
3 tablespoons honey
275ml/½ pint natural yoghurt

---

1 Separate the lettuce leaves and use to line the bottom of 4 individual plates. Remove the seeds from the melon and chop the flesh into cubes. Peel the grapefruit and orange, removing all the pith and cut into segments.

---

2 Place the melon, grapefruit and orange in a bowl and add the grapes, strawberries and raspberries. Mix well. Divide the fruit between the prepared plates. Mix together the honey and yoghurt only slightly, so that swirls of honey are visible in the mixture. Spoon over each salad and sprinkle with the toasted wheatgerm.

Serving suggestion: Decorate each plate with a sprig of red currants to serve.

Red Currant Soup

Serves 4—6   Preparation time: 15 minutes   Cooking time: 15 minutes

This sweet soup served cold is ideal for a hot summer's day.

450g/1lb fresh red currants,
  topped and tailed
100g/4oz sugar
25g/1oz flour
250ml/9fl oz Greek yoghurt

---

1   In a saucepan cook the red currants with the sugar and enough water just
    to cover the bottom of the pan, until the fruit is soft. Using a blender or food
    processor, purée the mixture until smooth and pass through a fine sieve.

---

2   Blend 2 tablespoons of the purée with the flour and then mix in with the remain-
    ing mixture. Place back into the saucepan and simmer gently, stirring until
    the soup thickens slightly.

Serving suggestion: Cool before serving. Serve in individual bowls with a dollop
or swirl of yoghurt.

Variations: The red currants can be replaced by black currants, gooseberries
or rhubarb, but adjust the quantity of sugar to taste.

Fruit Cream Mould

Serves 6   Preparation time: 30 minutes   Setting time: 3 hours

For the mould:
225g/8oz raspberries, hulled
225g/8oz red currants, topped
  and tailed
275ml/½ pint water
3 tablespoons sugar
25g/1oz powdered gelatine
275ml/½ pint double cream
1½ tablespoons sugar

For the decoration:
575ml/1 pint raspberry jelly
Fresh raspberries

---

1   Place the raspberries and red currants in a saucepan with the water and sugar and poach until the fruit is tender and the sugar dissolved. Drain the fruit and pass through a fine sieve. Measure 225ml/½ pint of the syrup and set it aside.

---

2   Line an 18cm/7in charlotte mould with the cold but still liquid jelly and set in the bottom the fresh raspberries for decoration. Spoon enough additional jelly on top of the decoration to cover and place in the refrigerator to set.

---

3   Soak the gelatine in half the reserved syrup in a saucepan and then set over a low heat and allow the gelatine to dissolve. In a bowl whip the cream until just thick and then fold in the fruit purée, 1½ tablespoons sugar and the remaining syrup. Set the fruit cream over a bowl full of ice and then add the gelatine mixture gradually stirring until it begins to thicken. Spoon into the prepared mould and place in the refrigerator to set.

Serving suggestion: Turn out of the mould and serve individual portions with fresh cream.

Summer Pudding

Serves 4—6   Preparation time: 40 minutes   Chilling time: 6 hours

The wonderfully versatile aspect of this heavenly pudding is that you can really use any soft summer fruit that is available.

450g/1lb raspberries or
  strawberries, hulled
225g/8oz black currants, topped
  and tailed
225g/8oz red currants, topped
  and tailed
100g/4oz blackberries, hulled
225g/8oz sugar
1 loaf white bread, sliced, with
  crusts removed
Fresh cream to serve

---

1   To prepare the mould, grease a 1.1 litre/2 pint pudding basin. Place the fruit in a separate bowl and add the sugar dissolved in a little water. Stir the fruit very gently and then place the bowl over a pan of simmering water to allow the sugar to dissolve and the juices to run.

---

2   Line the bottom and sides of the greased basin with 10 slices of bread so that they fit closely together.

---

3   Spoon one-third of the fruit into the lined basin and top with a slice of bread cut round to fit. Continue this layering, finishing with a layer of bread. Place a plate on top, with heavy weight to press the fruit down, and chill in the refrigerator for at least 6 hours to allow the juices to soak thoroughly into the bread.

Serving suggestion: Serve turned out on to a serving dish with dollops of fresh cream.

Variation: Instead of using slices of bread to line the summer pudding, try using slices of trifle sponge or cake.

Currant Sorbet

Serves 4—6   Preparation time: 25 minutes   Setting time: 4 hours

You may use either black or red currants for this recipe.

225g/8oz black or red currants
100g/4oz sugar
150ml/¼ pint whipping cream
150ml/¼ pint natural yoghurt
15g/½oz powdered gelatine
1 egg white, stiffly beaten
Fresh currants to garnish

1   Using a blender or food processor, purée the currants until smooth and then press through a fine sieve. Mix in the sugar, adjusting to taste and fold in the cream and yoghurt. Place the gelatine in a bowl set over a pan of hot water and dissolve in 1 tablespoon water. Set aside to cool slightly then beat into the fruit mixture.

2   Spoon into a freezer container, cover and place in the freezer. When the mixture is beginning to set, fold in the stiffly beaten egg white. Return to the freezer and mix once more before completely frozen. Freeze until firm.

Serving suggestion: Allow to soften slightly at room temperature before serving. Decorate with fresh currants.

Currant Roly-poly

Serves 4—6   Preparation time: 30 minutes   Cooking time: 1½ hours

For the base:
225g/8oz self-raising flour
½ teaspoon salt
100g/4oz shredded suet
8 tablespoons cold water

For the filling:
450g/1lb red or black currants,
  topped and tailed
175g/6oz sugar
1 tablespoon grated orange rind
Sugar to dredge
Custard to serve

Microwave: Follow the method as described and wrap loosely in cling-film. Cook on power 8 for 10 minutes and leave to stand for 5 minutes before serving.

1   Mix together the flour, salt and suet in a bowl. Add enough cold water to form an elastic dough and knead until smooth. Roll out into a rectangle 5mm/¼in thick.

2   Place the currants in a bowl. Mix together with the sugar and orange rind until thoroughly coated. Spread the mixture over the rectangle of pastry. Brush the edges with a little water and roll up from the longest side, Swiss roll fashion. Wrap in foil, sealing well as no water must get into the pastry.

3   Fill a saucepan with water and bring to the boil. Place the roll in a steamer set above the boiling water, cover, and steam for 1½ hours. Do not allow the pan to boil dry.

4   Lift out of the steamer and leave to stand for a few minutes before unwrapping.

Serving suggestion: Remove the wrapping and serve hot, dredged with sugar and with plenty of hot custard.

Soft Fruit Gateau

Serves 8   Preparation time: 20 minutes   Baking time: 1½ hours

For the cake:
225g/8oz butter
225g/8oz sugar
4 eggs, beaten
225g/8oz self-raising flour
Grated rind of 1 lemon
25g/1oz icing sugar
Sprigs of red currants to garnish

For the filling:
275ml/½ pint double cream
350g/12oz mixed soft fruit (red
  currants, raspberries, black
  currants, etc.), trimmed
75g/3oz sugar

Pre-heat the oven to 180°C/450°F/Gas Mark 4.

---

1   Grease and line 2 × 20cm/8in sandwich tins with greaseproof paper.

---

2   Cream together the butter and sugar until light and fluffy. Beat in the eggs one at a time and then fold in the flour with the lemon rind. Spoon into the prepared tins and bake for 1½ hours. Cool on a wire rack.

---

3   Whip the cream until thick. Place the fruit in a bowl and carefully mix in the sugar. Use the most level of the 2 cake layers as the base and spread with the whipped cream. Top with the fruit mixture and position the second sandwich layer on top.

Serving suggestion: Dust with the icing sugar and garnish with sprigs of red currant. Chill well before serving.

Spicy Red Bread

Makes 1 loaf   Preparation time: 20 minutes   Cooking time: 1 hour 10 minutes

150g/5oz fresh red or black
  currants
1 tablespoon sugar
225g/8oz sugar
2 tablespoons margarine
1 egg
175g/6oz self-raising flour
1 teaspoon bicarbonate of soda
1 teaspoon mixed spice

Pre-heat the oven to 180°C/350°F/Gas Mark 4.

---

1   Place the currants in a saucepan with 1 tablespoon of water and the tablespoon of sugar. Bring to simmering point and simmer until the fruit is softened and the juices run. Strain the currants and reserve the juice.

---

2   In a bowl, cream the sugar and margarine. Add the egg, mix well and then add the currants, 100ml/4fl oz reserved juice (made up with water if necessary) and 100ml/4fl oz water.

---

3   Into a separate bowl sift the flour with the bicarbonate of soda and spices and mix into the currant mixture. Grease and flour a 450g/1lb loaf tin. Pour in the mixture and bake for 1 hour 10 minutes.

---

4   When the bread is cooked, allow to cool a little, then remove from the loaf tin to cool completely on a wire rack.

Serving suggestion: Serve thinly sliced and spread with cream cheese.

Freezing: This loaf will freeze for up to 3 months.

Currant Compote

Serves 4   Preparation time: 2—3 hours   Chilling time: 2—3 hours

450g/1lb red or black currants or
  mixed
4 tablespoons black currant
  cordial
4 tablespoons lemon juice
4 tablespoons dark rum
4 tablespoons icing sugar
225ml/8fl oz whipping cream,
  whipped
Sweet plain biscuits to serve

1   Wash, top and tail the currants. Place the fruit in a bowl and pour over the
    black currant cordial, lemon juice and rum and mix together carefully.

2   Sprinkle with the sugar, cover and chill in the refrigerator for 2—3 hours,
    stirring occasionally.

Serving suggestion: Serve in individual bowls topped with whipped cream and
accompanied by sweet biscuits.

Trout with Currant Butter

Serves 4 as a main course, or 8 as a starter   Preparation time: 2 hours
Cooking time: 30 minutes

For the fish:
4 fresh trout
Fish stock for poaching

For the butter:
125ml/4fl oz raspberry vinegar
  (see note)
75ml/3fl oz white wine
6 tablespoons finely chopped
  spring onions
2 tablespoons fresh orange juice
350g/12oz cold butter
Salt and freshly ground black
  pepper
100g/4oz red or black currants,
  lightly poached in very little
  water to soften
Watercress to garnish

1   First poach the trout in the fish stock until just opaque. This may be done
     2 hours ahead, in which case allow the fish to stand in the poaching liquid
     until ready to use. Remove the skin from the fish, cut down the upper edge
     and lift off the flesh, removing the bones.

2   To make the sauce, simmer the vinegar, wine, spring onions and orange juice
     until the mixture is reduced to 2 tablespoons (20 minutes). Bring to the boil,
     remove from the heat and beat in 2 tablespoons of the butter. Over a very
     low heat beat in the remaining butter, 1 tablespoon at a time, being very careful
     the sauce does not break down. Remove from the heat, season with salt and
     pepper. Drain the currants and add to the butter sauce.

Serving suggestion: Spoon a little sauce on to each plate and place the trout
on top. Serve with a salad.

122

Note: Raspberry vinegar can be found in most speciality food shops, or make your own following this simple recipe:

1.1 litres/2 pints raspberries, hulled
1.1 litres/2 pints white wine vinegar
Sugar (see below)

1   Pour the vinegar over the raspberries and leave standing for 4 days. Strain and add 450g/1lb sugar to every 1.1 litres/2 pints liquid. Place in a saucepan and heat until just simmering.

2   Allow to cool, pour into bottles and cork tightly. Store in a cool, dry place.

Frozen Currant Meringue Gateau

Serves 6   Preparation time: 3 ½ hours   Setting time: 4 hours

This dish is so easy to make, it's wicked!

225g/8oz black or red currants,
  trimmed
2 tablespoons kirsch
2 tablespoons sugar
300ml/½ pint double cream
1 quantity meringue (see page
  58) or 12 shop-bought
  meringue shells
Whipped cream and fresh
  currants to decorate

---

1   Allow the currants to marinate in the kirsch for 3 hours, turning frequently. Place in a blender or food processor and purée with the sugar. Press the mixture through a fine sieve into a bowl. Whip the cream until thick and fold into the fruit mixture.

---

2   Break the meringue into pieces and fold into the fruit cream, but be careful to leave the mixture with a marbled effect. Spoon into an 18cm/7in springform tin. Cover and freeze for at least 4 hours.

Serving suggestion: Turn out the gateau on to a serving dish and allow to soften slightly. Serve decorated with whipped cream and fresh currants.

Black Currant Ice-cream Cake

Serves 4—6   Preparation time: 30 minutes   Freezing time: 4 hours

For the ice-cream:
*225g/8oz black currants, topped
  and tailed*
100g/4oz sugar
2 tablespoons cassis
3 tablespoons water
4 eggs, separated
*275ml/½pint double cream,
  whipped*
*Sprigs of black currants to
  garnish*

For the base:
2 large shop-bought jam rolls
3 tablespoons cassis

*Raspberry sauce to serve
  (see page 64)*

---

1   First prepare the ice-cream. Place the black currants, sugar, cassis and water into a saucepan and bring gently to the boil, stirring until the sugar has dissolved. Cook until the fruit is soft, then press it through a fine sieve to make a thick purée. Beat together the egg yolks, cream and purée. Whisk the egg whites until stiff and then fold into the black currant mixture.

---

2   Line the base of an 18cm/7in charlotte mould with cooking foil. Slice the jam rolls into rounds, dip each into the cassis and use to line the base and sides of the mould, trimming if necessary for a good fit. Pour in half the ice-cream mixture and cover the top with a single layer of any remaining dipped rounds. Pour in the remaining ice-cream mixture and freeze until firm.

Serving suggestion: Carefully turn out the mould on to a serving dish and remove the foil. Allow to soften slightly in the refrigerator before serving. Serve with raspberry sauce and garnished with fresh black currants.

Freezing: The ice-cream will keep in the freezer for up to 3 months.

CHAPTER 6

EXOTIC GARDEN FRUITS

During the seventeenth century, tremendous energy and enterprise went into the cultivation of a large range and variety of fruits that we tend now to regard as exotics, expecting to buy them in the shops rather than grow them ourselves. Gardeners of the past skilfully tended these fruit trees that were used to the warmth of Southern Europe, and much of what we know today about growing fruits such as grapes, peaches, apricots, nectarines and figs is a direct gift from our ancestors of three centuries ago.

The apricot was first introduced from Italy in about 1542 by John Woolf, gardener to Henry VIII, and within twenty years was widely cultivated around the country. Gardeners of old not only loved the apricots and peaches for their delicious fruits, but also for their beautiful flowers.

'The beautiful show of these... sorts of flowers hath made them into this garden in that for their worthiness I am unwilling to be without them, although the rest of their kindes I have transferred into the orchard.'

So wrote John Parkinson, a gardener of the seventeenth century.

Peaches and nectarines are, surprisingly enough, of the same species, although the nectarine is slightly more tender than its richly flavoured cousin. Fine, ripe peaches and nectarines travel badly, as they bruise easily, so those sold at the market are selected for early picking and good keeping qualities. Sadly, unless we grow our own, we never get the chance to taste the sun-ripened varieties with the best flavours.

Over the years, the wide variety of figs available has diminished to just a few, the two best types being the large, well-flavoured Brown Turkey and the Brunswick. The Fig has been enjoyed since the reign of Edward I for its beautiful trees and rich, heavenly fruit. Similarly enjoyed has been the grape, the main role of which has been to provide us with wine. All the grapes of today are descended from the wild grape-vine. Grapes became particularly popular as a dessert fruit all over Europe during the seventeenth century when glasshouses first appeared. The muscat, which appears in the shops all the year round, is considered the most elegant of all.

Orange and Apricot Chicken

Serves 6   Preparation time: see below   Cooking time: 30 minutes

Marinate this dish overnight in the refrigerator for best results.

350ml/12fl oz fresh orange juice
225g/8oz apricot preserve
3 tablespoons chopped fresh
  ginger
2 tablespoons sesame oil
2 tablespoons wholegrain
  mustard
1 tablespoon grated lemon and
  orange rind
4 cloves
6 boneless chicken breasts
Boiled rice to serve

---

1   In a blender or food processor, blend together the orange juice, apricot preserve, ginger, oil, mustard, lemon and orange rind and cloves until creamy. Arrange the chicken in a roasting tin and spoon over the orange mixture. Cover and refrigerate overnight.

Pre-heat the oven to 200°C/400°F/Gas Mark 6.

---

2   Remove the chicken from the marinade and place in another roasting tin. Cook, basting frequently with the marinade, until the chicken is cooked and golden brown (30 minutes).

Serving suggestion: Serve hot on a bed of boiled rice with a crisp salad or cooked vegetables.

Lamb Kebabs

Serves 4   Preparation time: see below   Cooking time: 25 minutes

Try these tasty kebabs next time you plan an outdoor barbecue.

450g/1lb lamb fillets, cubed
2 cloves garlic, crushed
4 tablepoons olive oil
Salt and freshly ground black
  pepper
1 teaspoon dried mint
275ml/½ pint natural yoghurt
2 small onions, cut into chunks
2 green or red peppers, seeded
  and cut into chunks
2 apricots, stoned and cut into
  chunks
Lemon wedges to garnish

1   Place the lamb in a bowl and sprinkle over the garlic, oil, salt pepper and
    mint. Pour over the yoghurt and leave to marinate in the refrigerator for 4
    hours, turning the meat occasionally.

2   After 4 hours, thread the lamb on to 4 or 8 well oiled skewers, alternating
    with chunks of onion, pepper and apricot. Either set on a hot barbecue or
    under a pre-heated hot grill for 25 minutes, or until the lamb is tender and
    cooked. Turn the skewers during cooking and baste with a little marinade.

Serving suggestion: Serve with wedges of lemon on a bed of rice with a crisp
salad.

Cold Curry and Apricot Soup

Serves 4   Preparation time: 30 minutes   Chilling time: 4 hours

25g/1oz butter
100g/4oz finely-chopped spring
  onions
1 tablespoon and 1 teaspoon
  curry paste
25g/1oz flour
1.1 litre/2 pints chicken stock
1 teaspoon grated lemon rind
1 bay-leaf
1 tablespoon arrowroot, dissolved
  in 1 tablespoon water
2 apricots, peeled and stoned
1 wine glass port
150ml/¼ pint double cream

1   Melt the butter in a frying pan and gently cook the spring onions until
    transparent. Add the tablespoon curry paste and stir over the heat for 5
    minutes. Add the flour, stir well, then slowly add the stock, stirring all the
    time. Bring to the boil, add the lemon rind and bay-leaf and simmer,
    uncovered, for 20 minutes.

2   Pass the soup through a fine sieve, return to the saucepan and add the soaked
    arrowroot. Bring to the boil, stirring until thickened. Chill thoroughly in the
    refrigerator while making the apricot purée.

3   Chop the apricots and place in a saucepan with the port. Simmer, uncovered,
    until the apricots are very soft, then press through a fine sieve to produce
    a purée. Return to the pan and add the teaspoon curry paste, simmering until
    reduced by half. Leave to cool. Whip the cream until just thick and then beat
    into the apricot mixture.

Serving suggestion: Serve the soup and the cream mixture separately.

Freezing: This soup will keep for up to 1 week in the freezer.

Orange, Apricot and Yoghurt Soup

Serves 6   Preparation time: 15 minutes   Chilling time: 1 hour

This is an exotic soup served cold on hot summer days.

4—6 apricots, stoned
450ml/16fl oz natural yoghurt
2 tablespoons sugar
225ml/8fl oz milk
125ml/4fl oz fresh orange juice
1 orange, peeled and very thinly
  sliced
6 sprigs fresh mint to garnish

1   Place the apricots, yoghurt and sugar in a blender or food processor and purée. Press through a fine sieve. Combine the purée with the milk and orange juice, mixing well.

2   Cover and chill in the refrigerator for at least 1 hour.

Serving suggestion: Serve the soup in individual glasses garnished with a thin slice of orange and a fresh sprig of mint.

Freezing: This soup will keep for 1 week in the freezer.

Apricot Squares

Makes 30   Preparation time: 30 minutes   Cooking time: 20 minutes

175g/6oz oatmeal
100g/4oz apricots, peeled, stoned
 and chopped
225g/8oz plain flour
225g/8oz butter or margarine
100g/4oz soft brown sugar
1½ teaspoons cinnamon
½ teaspoon bicarbonate of soda
225g/8oz apricot preserves

Pre-heat the oven to 200°C/400°F/Gas Mark 6.

1   Grease a 23 × 35cm/9 × 14in baking dish. In a bowl mix together the oatmeal, chopped apricots, flour, butter, sugar, cinnamon and soda, rubbing in until crumbly.

2   Press half the mixture into the bottom of the prepared dish. Spread the preserves over and crumble the remaining oat mixture on to the top. Bake until golden brown (20 minutes).

Serving suggestion: Serve cut into squares as a snack or tea-time treat.

Deep-dish Apricot and Peach Pie

Serves 6   Preparation time: 40 minutes   Baking time: 50 minutes

For the pastry:
350g/12oz plain flour
Pinch of salt
175g/6oz fat, half lard and half
  butter

For the filling:
700g/1½lb peaches
450g/1lb apricots

50g/1oz butter
100g/4oz sugar
15g/½oz cornflour
½ teaspoon cinnamon
50g/2oz sliced almonds (optional)
Beaten egg to glaze
Sugar to sprinkle
Vanilla ice-cream to serve

1 Make the pastry by sifting the flour with the salt into a bowl. Cup up the fat into cubes and add the flour. Using just fingertips, rub the fat into the flour until the mixture resembles fine breadcrumbs. Slowly add enough cold water to form a stiff dough, mixing with a round-bladed knife. Knead lightly for 15 minutes.

Pre-heat the oven to 220°C/425°F/Gas Mark 7.

2 Roll out three-quarters of the pastry to line a 25 × 20cm/10 × 8in oven-proof dish. Peel, stone and slice the peaches and apricots and arrange in the dish. Dot with butter. Mix together the sugar, cornflour and cinnamon (and almonds if using), and sprinkle over the peaches. Roll out the remaining pastry and cut to form a lattice on top. Dampen the edges and press down firmly. Brush with beaten egg.

3 Bake for 40 minutes and then sprinkle the top with a little sugar and bake for a further 10 minutes.

Serving suggestion: Serve hot with vanilla ice-cream.

Apricot and Mint Stuffed Lamb

Serves 6   Preparation time: 25 minutes   Cooking time: 1½ hours

1.5kg/4lb leg of lamb, boned and
trimmed
Salt and freshly ground black
pepper
40g/1½ oz butter
1 small onion, finely chopped
100g/4oz fresh breadcrumbs

2 teaspoons freshly chopped
parsley
1 teaspoon freshly chopped mint
100g/4oz dried apricots, chopped
150ml/¼ pint stock
25g/1oz lard
275ml/½ pint water

Pre-heat the oven to 180°C/350°F/Gas Mark 4.

Microwave: To cook this stuffed leg of lamb in the microwave, prepare as described. Before cooking, brush the joint with melted butter and cover with roasting film or greaseproof paper. Cook on power 9 for 2 minutes per 450g/1lb, then reduce to power 7 and continue cooking for 7 minutes per 450g/1lb. Remove the roasting film half-way through cooking, turn the joint and baste with the juices. Leave to stand, wrapped in foil, for about 15 minutes before carving.

1   First season the lamb thoroughly with salt and pepper and put to one side.

2   In a frying pan, melt the butter and sauté the onion for 2 minutes. Add the breadcrumbs, parsley, mint and apricots and enough stock to make the mixture stiff. Season to taste. Spoon the mixture into the boned cavity, packing down, and sew up using fine string and a trussing needle.

3   In a large casserole, heat the lard and brown the meat all over. Add the water and bring to the boil. Cover the casserole and place in the oven to bake for 1½ hours, basting occasionally.

Serving suggestion: Place the lamb on a serving dish and pour over the juices. Serve immediately with creamy mashed potatoes and broccoli.

Chicken Curry

Serves 4   Preparation time: 30 minutes   Cooking time: 35 minutes

This dish is extremely versatile and really any fresh fruit can be used depending on the season. If the fresh fruit of your choice is not available, try using dried apricots, prunes, or even dried peaches.

2 tablespoons desiccated coconut
150ml/¼ pint boiling water
1 large onion, thinly sliced
50g/2oz butter or margarine
2 tablespoons flour
1 tablespoon curry powder
1 teaspoon coriander seeds,
  crushed
2 small pieces fresh ginger,
  finely chopped
575ml/1 pint chicken stock
450g/1lb apricots or peaches,
  peeled, cored and chopped
400g/14oz cooked chicken meat,
  chopped
6 tablespoons double cream or
  thick Greek yoghurt
1 tablespoon fresh lemon juice
Salt and freshly ground black
  pepper

---

1   Soak the coconut in boiling water and put it aside. In a frying pan fry the onion in the butter until soft and then stir in the flour, curry powder, coriander and ginger. Stir over the heat for 5 minutes. Strain the coconut water and add to the spice mixture with the stock. Simmer for 20 minutes.

---

2   Add the fruit to the curry, stirring well. Then add the chicken and simmer for a further 10 minutes. Add the cream or yoghurt, lemon juice and seasoning.

Serving suggestion: Serve hot with boiled rice.

Peach Melba Ice-cream

Serves 6   Preparation time: 30 minutes   Freezing time: 4 hours

A slight variation on the traditional Peach Melba dessert using a lovely creamy peach ice-cream.

For the shells and topping:
6 individual meringue nests
Raspberry sauce (see page 64)

For the ice-cream:
5 ripe peaches, peeled, stoned
  and chopped
275g/10oz sugar
3 level tablespoons plain flour
½ teaspoon salt
575ml/1 pint milk
3 eggs, beaten
425ml/¾ pint double cream
½ teaspoon almond essence
Whipped cream to serve

1   In a blender or food processor, purée the peaches with 50g/2oz of the sugar. Put aside. In a large saucepan, mix the remaining sugar with the flour and salt. Beat the milk with the eggs and stir into the sugar mixture until smooth. Place over a low heat, stirring continuously, until the custard thickens (15 minutes). Chill.

2   Stir in the peach purée, double cream and almond essence. Pour into a rigid freezer container, cover and freeze for 4 hours.

3   Spoon into a bowl and beat until smooth. Return to the freezer in a covered container and freeze until firm.

Serving suggestion: Just before serving, allow the ice cream to soften slightly at room temperature. Spoon equal amounts of ice cream into the meringue nests and pour over the raspberry sauce. Serve with whipped cream.

Baked Stuffed Peaches

Serves 4   Preparation time: 20 minutes   Cooking time: 30—40 minutes

4 large peaches, peeled, halved
* and stoned*
4 heaped tablespoons raisins
½ teaspoon ground ginger
125ml/4fl oz sweetened
* condensed milk*
4 tablespoons sherry
100g/4oz soft brown sugar
225ml/8fl oz soured cream

Pre-heat the oven to 180°C/350°F/Gas Mark 4.

1   Place the peach halves on a shallow baking dish. If necessary, using a small spoon, scoop out a little of the cavity left by the stone to hold more stuffing. Mix together the raisins and ginger and press into the cavities.

2   Mix together the condensed milk and sherry and pour over the peaches. Place in the oven and bake for 30—40 minutes until the peaches are tender, basting occasionally with the juices. Remove and allow to cool. Sprinkle the brown sugar over the peaches and place under a hot grill until the sugar has caramelised — just a few minutes. Do not allow the sugar to burn. Chill in the refrigerator and serve with the juices.

Serving suggestion: Serve with soured cream.

Peach Crème Brûlée

Serves 6   Preparation time: 20 minutes   Cooking time: 15 minutes
Chilling time: 3 hours

Crème Brûlée is a luxurious dessert that ought to be worshipped. With the addition of sweet, soft peaches set at the bottom of each ramekin, who can resist it?

4—6 ripe peaches
Sugar for sprinkling
425ml/¾ pint double cream
1 vanilla pod, slightly bruised
4 egg yolks
1 tablespoon caster sugar
Soft brown sugar for topping

1   Bring a saucepan of water to the boil and drop in the peaches for 10 seconds. Remove from the water, peel, stone and slice. Divide between 6 individual ramekin dishes, sprinkle with a little sugar and put aside.

2   Put the cream in a saucepan with the vanilla pod and bring to scalding point. Do not allow to boil. Remove from the heat.

3   In a bowl, beat the egg yolks with the sugar until light and slightly thickened. Pour in the cream very slowly, stirring all the time until well combined. Place in a saucepan set over a pan of simmering water. Stir until the mixture coats the back of a spoon, then pour into the ramekin dishes over the peaches.

4   Chill thoroughly in the refrigerator. When the *crème* has set, sprinkle each with 5mm/¼ in layer of brown sugar. Set the grill to very hot and place the dishes under it until the sugar caramelises. Remove and allow to cool.

Serving suggestion: Serve chilled. Before serving, gently crack the crisp sugar top.

Pork with Peaches

Serves 6   Preparation time: 30 minutes   Cooking time: 20 minutes

It's the apricot brandy that really makes this dish stand out!

900g/2½lb pork tenderloin,
  trimmed and cut into 20 pieces
Plain flour to dredge
Salt and freshly ground black
  pepper
Oil for frying
125ml/4fl oz apricot brandy
225ml/8fl oz stock
225g/8oz unsalted butter
2 peaches, peeled and sliced in
  wedges
¼ teaspoon allspice
¼ teaspoon nutmeg
¼ teaspoon cinnamon

1   Pat the pork pieces dry with kitchen paper. Put the flour and seasoning into a plastic bag and, placing the pork into the bag a few pieces at a time, completely coat each one, shaking off any excess.

2   In a large frying pan heat a thin layer of oil and fry the pork on all sides until cooked through, turning frequently. Remove from the pan and keep warm on a serving dish. Pour off any excess oil in the pan and add the brandy. Heat and *flambé*, then add the stock. Boil the mixture until it reduces by two-thirds, remove from the heat and add 2 tablespoons of the butter, beating in well.

3   Return to the heat adding the remaining butter, 1 tablespoon at a time. Add the peaches and heat through, then add the remaining spices.

Serving suggestion: Pour the peach sauce over the pork and serve with buttered noodles and fresh vegetables.

Wine-poached Figs

Serves 4   Preparation time: 15 minutes   Cooking time: 20 minutes

175g/6oz fresh raspberries or
  frozen and thawed
350ml/12fl oz dry red wine
150g/5oz sugar
2 tablespoons fresh lemon juice
12 fresh figs
Thick Greek yoghurt to serve

1   Using a blender or food processor, purée the raspberries and pass through a fine sieve to remove all the seeds. Put the purée in a saucepan, add the wine, sugar and lemon juice and cook slowly until the sugar has dissolved.

2   Bring the heat up to simmering point and add the figs. Simmer for 15 minutes. Remove with a perforated spoon and boil the mixture until it is reduced to 175ml/6fl oz.

Serving suggestion: Divide the figs between 4 individual dishes and pour the raspberry sauce over. Chill thoroughly before serving. Serve with thick Greek yoghurt.

Note: Tinned or dried figs may be substituted for fresh but be careful when poaching and make sure that the figs do not become mushy.

Fresh Figs in Port

Serves 4   Preparation time: 40 minutes   Chilling time: 20 minutes

Fresh figs are truly the food of the gods! This heavenly dish is ideal served at any time.

450g/1lb fresh ripe figs
150ml/¼ pint port
50ml/2fl oz thick Greek yoghurt
50ml/2fl oz single cream
Sprig of mint to garnish

---

1   Carefully peel and slice the figs and place in a shallow bowl. Add the port, cover in cling-film and chill in the refrigerator for 20 minutes.

---

2   Combine the yoghurt with the cream and pour over the figs. Stir gently before serving.

Serving suggestion: Garnish with a sprig of mint and serve in individual dishes.

Fig Tart with Raspberries

Serves 6—8   Preparation time: 45 minutes   Chilling time: 10 hours

For the tart:
12 large fresh figs
125ml/4fl oz kirsch
1 quantity rich pastry (see page 32)
225g/8oz raspberries, hulled

For the cream:
225ml/8fl oz milk
50g/2oz sugar
2 tablespoons plain flour
1 egg yolk
2 teaspoons unsalted butter
1 teaspoon vanilla essence

For the glaze:
3 tablespoons red currant jelly (see page 112)
1 tablespoon kirsch

1   First make the pastry cream. In a saucepan scald the milk, and while the milk is heating up, mix the sugar and flour together in a bowl. When the milk is ready, remove the skin and add to the sugar and flour, beating continuously. Place the bowl over a saucepan of simmering water and stir constantly for about 10 minutes. Add the egg yolk and stir continuously until the mixture coats the back of a spoon (10 minutes). Remove from the heat. Add the butter and vanilla, mix well and chill.

2   Peel the figs and cut them in half. Place in a bowl, pour over the kirsch and leave in the refrigerator for 10 hours, stirring occasionally.

3   Prepare the pastry, and use it to line a 23cm/9in pie dish. Bake blind according to the directions, and allow to cool. Spread the tart cream in the base of the cooled pastry shell. Drain the figs and arrange, cut side down, on the cream. Fill all the spaces with the raspberries. Make the red currant glaze by mixing the red currant jelly and kirsch together over a medium heat until smooth. Brush all over the fruit in the tart.

Serving suggestion: Serve immediately with whipped cream.

Sole Veronique

Serves 4—6   Preparation time: 25 minutes   Cooking time: 30 minutes

This classic recipe combines the subtle flavours of fresh sole with a light creamy sauce and sweet, juicy grapes.

For the fish:
6 × 100g/4oz sole fillets
Salt and freshly ground white
  pepper
1 onion, thinly sliced
1 bay-leaf
200ml/7fl oz dry white wine
125ml/4fl oz water
175g/6oz green, seedless grapes
Fresh parsley to garnish

For the sauce:
25g/1oz butter
25g/1oz flour
Salt and freshly ground white
  pepper
125ml/4fl oz milk or single
  cream

Pre-heat the oven to 180°C/350°F/Gas Mark 4.
Microwave: To cook the sole in the microwave, arrange the fillets in a shallow dish with a lid with the thinner or smaller ends facing the centre. Continue as below, cover the dish and cook on power 7 for 4—5 minutes per 450g/1lb. Allow to stand for 3 minutes before serving.

---

1   Arrange the fish fillets on the bottom of a lightly-greased baking dish. Season with salt and pepper, add the sliced onion and crushed bay-leaf and pour over the wine and water. Cover with foil and bake for 15—20 minutes until the fish is cooked.

---

2   Remove the fish from the baking dish using a perforated spoon and keep warm. Strain the cooking juices and reserve 100ml/4fl oz of the stock.

---

3   To make the sauce, melt the butter in a saucepan and stir in the flour. Stir over the heat for 1 minute, season and then gradually add the milk or cream and reserved stock. Season again and stir over the heat until the sauce thickens (2 minutes). Stir in the grapes.

Serving suggestion: To serve, place the fish fillets on a serving dish, pour over the grape sauce and garnish with fresh parsley.

Prawn and Grape Salad

Serves 6 as a main course, 8 as a starter   Preparation time: 15 minutes
Chilling time: 4 hours

This attractive dish is equally delicious and popular as a first course, main course or luncheon dish.

225ml/8fl oz soured cream
225ml/8fl oz mayonnaise
700g/2lb cooked peeled prawns
225g/8oz green seedless grapes
25g/1oz fresh dill
Salt and freshly ground black
  pepper
Crisp lettuce to serve

1   In a bowl beat together the soured cream and mayonnaise thoroughly. Pour the dressing over the prawns, toss, add the grapes and toss gently again. Sprinkle on the fresh dill, season to taste and toss.

2   Cover and chill thoroughly in the refrigerator for 4 hours.

Serving suggestion: Just before serving, adjust seasoning and toss again. Serve arranged on lettuce leaves on individual plates.

Macaroni Grape Salad

Serves 4   Preparation time: 30 minutes

This yoghurt salad dressing is really so easy and is ideal with any salad.

For the salad:
225g/8oz macaroni shells
350g/12oz cooked ham, cut into
  strips
225g/8oz green seedless grapes
75g/3oz celery, chopped
½ honeydew melon
1 head lettuce

For the dressing:
150ml/¼ pint yoghurt
½ teaspoon paprika
2 tablespoons chopped chives
Salt and freshly ground black
  pepper
2 teaspoons vinegar

---

1   Cook the pasta in a saucepan of lightly-salted water until just cooked. Drain. In a bowl combine the macaroni with the ham, grapes and celery. Make the salad dressing by combining all the ingredients together in the order given. Adjust seasoning to taste.

---

2   Combine half the salad dressing with the salad; cover and chill before serving.

Serving suggestion: To serve, peel and slice the melon and arrange on a serving dish with the lettuce. Top with the macaroni salad and serve with the additional salad dressing.

Grape-stuffed Avocados

Serves 6—8   Preparation time: 15 minutes   Chilling time: 4 hours

A light buffet dish, these avocados will also prove delightful as starters for a dinner party.

125ml/4fl oz soured cream
125ml/4fl oz mayonnaise
450g/1lb cooked prawns
175g/6oz green seedless grapes
15g/½oz freshly chopped dill
Salt and freshly ground pepper
3—4 avocados, halved and
  stoned
1 tablespoon lemon juice
Lettuce leaves to serve

1   In a small bowl beat the soured cream and mayonnaise together thoroughly. Add the prawns and toss gently. Add the grapes and toss well. Sprinkle on the dill and salt and pepper to taste. Toss, cover and refrigerate for at least 4 hours.

2   Just before serving, sprinkle the avocado halves with lemon juice to prevent discoloration. Adjust the seasoning of the prawn mixture, if necessary, and spoon into the cavity of each avocado half.

Serving suggestion: Serve on a bed of lettuce leaves.

Grape Mousse

Serves 4—6   Preparation time: 30 minutes   Chilling time: see below

Be a little adventurous using fresh herbs — they should not only be kept for savoury dishes.

1 tablespoon powdered gelatine
50ml/2fl oz cold water
350ml/12fl oz red grape juice
50g/2oz sugar
2 fresh thyme sprigs
½ teaspoon vanilla essence
225ml/8fl oz natural yoghurt
Green seedless grapes to garnish

1   Sprinkle the gelatine over the water in a bowl and leave for 10 minutes.

2   In a saucepan, bring the grape juice to simmering point, add the sugar and thyme and stir until the sugar is dissolved. Remove from the heat, add the vanilla and pour through a fine sieve. Beat the hot juice into the gelatine mixture until the gelatine is completely dissolved and place in the refrigerator for 1 hour until it just begins to thicken.

3   Beat the mixture again for 1 minute and then add the yoghurt. Dampen the inside of an 850ml/1½ pint jelly mould and pour in the mixture. Cover and chill overnight.

Serving suggestion: Remove the mousse from the mould by wrapping it in a hot, damp tea-towel and shaking gently. Invert on to a serving plate and garnish with fresh grapes.

Fried Chicken with Grapes

Serves 6   Preparation time: 15 minutes   Cooking time: 20 minutes

100g/4oz dried breadcrumbs
Salt and freshly ground black
  pepper
½ teaspoon dried tarragon
¼ teaspoon poultry seasoning
6 chicken breasts, boned
7 tablespoons butter
125ml/4fl oz chicken stock
125ml/4fl oz white wine
125ml/8oz mushrooms, sliced
225g/8oz green seedless grapes

Pre-heat the oven to 180°C/350°F/Gas Mark 4.

---

1   In a bowl combine the breadcrumbs, salt and pepper, tarragon and poultry seasoning. Coat each chicken breast thoroughly with this mixture. Melt 4 tablespoons of the butter in a large, heavy-based frying pan and brown the chicken on both sides. Place the chicken in a shallow roasting pan in a single layer.

---

2   In a saucepan bring the stock and wine to the boil and then pour it in around the chicken. Bake uncovered for 20 minutes.

---

3   Meanwhile sauté the mushrooms in the remaining butter. Add the mushrooms and grapes to the chicken and cook for a further 10 minutes.

Serving suggestion: Serve with creamy mashed potato and freshly cooked vegetables.

Top *Port and Plum Sorbet (page 96)*
Left *Peppers Stuffed with Prune Cream Cheese (page 100)*
Right *Deep-dish Plum Pie (page 86)*
Bottom *Devils on Horseback (page 97)*

Top *Blackcurrant Ice-cream Cake (page 125)*
Left *Spicy Red Bread (page 120)*
Right *Frozen Currant Meringue Gateau (page 124)*
Bottom *Game Pie (page 106)*

Top left *Sole Veronique (page 143)* **Top right** *Apricot Squares (page 132)*
Left *Lamb Kebabs (page 129)* **Right** *Peach Crème Brûlée (page 138)*

Top left *St Clement's Chequer-board Cake (page 164)*
Top right *Orange Oatmeal Biscuits (page 158)*
Left *Spicy Orange Shrimp (page 151)*
Right *Tuna Pâté Stuffed Lemons (page 162)*

CHAPTER 7

CITRUS DELIGHTS

The beautiful citrus fruit of the orange, lemon, lime and grapefruit have one thing in common — they ripen only whilst on the tree, and once they have been picked, their flavour does not improve, nor does it become any sweeter. These fruits come from warmer climates such as Italy, Spain and the Americas and they travel well, remain in good condition for several weeks, and reach our market stalls and supermarkets more or less as they left their trees.

There are three main types of orange to choose from: the thin-skinned, sweet Valencia type; the larger, thick-skinned seedless type; and the bitter Seville oranges. Although Britain cannot boast these particular fruits amongst its fruit growing successes, it was in Scotland that orange marmalade was first invented during the eighteenth century, when a boat-load of unexpectedly bitter Portuguese oranges arrived in Dundee.

Lemons are extremely rich in vitamin C and are indispensable to any cook. Large or small, smooth, thin-skinned or thick, knobbly-skinned, the lemon's juice and rind finds its way into puddings, cakes, pies, sauces, soups, salads and sorbets, and enhances and aids the cooking of other fruits.

Limes are probably the most perishable of the citrus fruits. Sharp and aromatic, they can be used for the same purposes as lemons, and their juice is an essential ingredient in many traditional drinks from their native countries, such as margharitas and daiquiris. Choose those with a pale or dark green skin, as those that have turned slightly yellow tend to have lost their tang.

The grapefruit has always been a very popular breakfast dish or starter. Yellow or pink, with the merest trace of bitterness, the grapefruit is a descendant of the Polynesian pomelo which arrived in the West Indies during the seventeenth century, thanks to an enterprising English sea captain. Mousses, cocktails, sorbets and salads all benefit from its unique qualities, but choose those that feel heavy for their size as this means there is plenty of juice.

Orange Pork Chops

Serves 6   Preparation time: 45 minutes   Cooking time: 45 minutes

6 pork loin chops
2 tablespoons oil
2 tablespoons flour
½ teaspoon salt
1 tablespoon brown sugar
Dash ground ginger
1 tablespoon grated orange rind
225ml/8fl oz fresh orange juice
2 oranges, peeled and segmented

1   Pat the pork chops dry with kitchen paper. Heat the oil in a large frying pan and brown the chops on both sides for 10 minutes each side.

2   Drain the fat. In a bowl, combine the remaining ingredients except the orange segments and pour over the chops. Cover, reduce the heat and simmer for 45 minutes until the chops are very tender. Just before serving, add the orange segments.

Serving suggestion: Serve on a bed of rice with freshly cooked vegetables.

Spicy Orange Shrimp

Serves 6—8   Preparation time: 20 minutes   Cooking time: 15 minutes

There is a slightly Oriental taste to this dish when served with boiled rice — you may feel inclined to use chopsticks.

3 large oranges
3 tablespoons oil
1 teaspoon crushed garlic
600g/1½lb uncooked shelled
  shrimp
2 tablespoons hot pepper sauce
1 tablespoon light brown sugar
1 tablespoon Worcestershire
  sauce
1 tablespoon cornflour, dissolved
  in 1 tablespoon cold water

1   Squeeze the juice of the oranges into a bowl, discarding any seeds and white pith. Heat the oil in a large frying pan or wok, add the garlic and cook for 1 minute.

2   Add the shrimp and stir fry until cooked and bright pink (1 minute). Add the hot pepper sauce, brown sugar and Worcestershire sauce. Stir well. Next add the orange juice and bring to the boil. Cook, stirring, for 2 minutes and then add the dissolved cornflour. Continue cooking for 3 minutes until the sauce thickens.

Serving suggestion: Serve immediately on a bed of rice.

Fruit Yoghurt Salad

Serves 6—8   Preparation time: 1½ hours   Cooking time: 4 minutes

This cooling salad is especially nice when served with spicier dishes. The ground cumin seeds are the final touch to this pink salad.

450ml/16fl oz natural yoghurt
1 large boiled potato, peeled and
  chopped
1 large orange, peeled and
  segmented
1 cooked beetroot, cubed
50g/2oz chopped walnuts
Salt and freshly ground black
  pepper
1 teaspoon cumin seeds

1   In a large bowl, mix together the yoghurt, potato, orange, beetroot and walnuts. Season with salt and pepper, cover and refrigerate for at least 1 hour.

2   Heat a small frying pan and add the cumin seeds. Toss on the heat for 4 minutes and do not allow to burn. Crush the toasted seeds to a powder using a pestle and mortar.

Serving suggestion: Serve the yoghurt salad with the cumin seeds sprinkled over the top.

Citrus Sole

Serves 4   Preparation time: 25 minutes   Cooking time: 20 minutes

The bonus to this dish is that it is very low in calories!

1 grapefruit
1 orange
100ml/4fl oz fresh orange juice
100ml/4fl oz fresh grapefruit
  juice
¼ teaspoon dried thyme
1 clove garlic, crushed
Salt and freshly ground black
  pepper
4 × 175g/6oz sole fillets
1 tablespoon fresh parsley, finely
  chopped

1   Using a very sharp knife, carefully remove only the coloured part of the rind
    from half the grapefruit and orange. Cut into very thin matchsticks and blanch
    in boiling water for 10 minutes. Drain, rinse under cold water and put aside.
    Segment the grapefruit and remove any white pith.

2   In a frying pan combine the orange and grapefruit juices, thyme, garlic and
    seasoning, and bring to the boil. Add the fish, cover loosely and simmer gently
    for 5 minutes, turning once, until the fish is just cooked through. Remove
    the fish to a large serving dish and keep warm. Bring the liquid to the boil
    and boil until reduced to a thin sauce consistency. Pour over the fish and
    garnish with the citrus matchsticks, grapefruit segments and fresh parsley.

Serving suggestion: Serve with French fries or a salad.

Carrot and Orange Soup

Serves 4   Preparation time: 20 minutes   Cooking time: 45 minutes

450g/1lb carrots, washed and
  peeled
50g/2oz butter
450g/1lb parsnips, peeled and
  thinly sliced
40g/1½oz flour
1.1 litres/2 pints chicken stock
1 bay-leaf
Salt and freshly ground black
  pepper
Juice of 2 oranges
Natural yoghurt to serve

---

1   Slice 100g/4oz of the carrots into thin matchsticks and reserve. Chop the remaining.

---

2   In a saucepan, melt the butter and add the chopped carrots and parsnips. Cook gently for 10 minutes, stirring. Add the flour and continue cooking for 1 minute. Gradually add the stock, stirring continuously. Add the bay-leaf, season to taste and simmer for 15—20 minutes until the vegetables are tender.

---

3   Remove the bay-leaf and, using a blender or food processor, purée the mixture. Return to the saucepan, add the matchstick carrots and orange juice and cover and simmer for a further 15 minutes until the carrots are tender.

Serving suggestion: Serve hot with a swirl of yoghurt.

Orange Surprise Chicken

Serves 6—8   Preparation time: 45 minutes

Here is a lovely tangy starter salad that also makes a terrific luncheon dish.

1 small cooked chicken
5 seedless oranges
1 green pepper, de-seeded and
  sliced
275ml/½ pint soured cream
275ml/½ pint thick Greek
  yoghurt
Dash paprika
Dash tabasco
1 teaspoon curry powder
1 teaspoon anchovy essence
Lettuce leaves to serve

1   First remove all the skin from the chicken and chop the flesh. Grate the rind of 4 of the oranges, reserving the remaining orange for garnish. Remove all the white pith and divide the orange into segments. Slice the remaining orange thinly and put aside.

2   Combine the chicken, orange rind, orange segments and sliced green pepper. Beat the soured cream and yoghurt together thoroughly in bowl, with the paprika, tabasco, curry powder and anchovy essence. Stir in the chicken mixture, cover and chill.

Serving suggestion: To serve, line individual plates with lettuce leaves and top with the orange chicken. Garnish with slices or orange.

Barbecued Spare-ribs

Serves 4   Preparation time: 30 minutes   Cooking time: 2 hours

This barbecue sauce is also great with chicken, hamburgers and hot dogs. Serve these spare-ribs with plenty of napkins as they are deliciously messy!

75ml/3fl oz vinegar
3 tablespoons brown sugar
1 tablespoon mustard
Salt and freshly ground black
  pepper
¼ teaspoon cayenne
½ lemon, thickly sliced
½ orange, thickly sliced
1 onion, sliced
75g/3oz butter or margarine
125ml/4fl oz tomato ketchup
3 tablespoons Worcestershire
  sauce
1.1kg/3lb spare-ribs, cut into
  serving pieces

Pre-heat the oven to 180°C/350°F/Gas Mark 4.
Microwave: It is best to seal the ribs under the grill before microwaving. Combine all the other ingredients in a large dish and cook on power 7 for 4 minutes. Stir and cook for a further 3 minutes on high power, stirring once. Place the ribs in the dish and spoon over the sauce. Cook on power 5 for about 20 minutes until the ribs are tender. Allow to stand before serving.

1   In a saucepan combine the first 9 ingredients. Mix well and simmer for 20 minutes, uncovered. Add the tomato ketchup and Worcestershire sauce and bring to the boil. Pat the spare-ribs dry with kitchen paper and brush all over with the sauce.

2   Place in a single layer in a shallow roasting tin and cook for 1½ hours, brushing frequently with the sauce and turning occasionally until all the ribs are tender.

Serving suggestion: Serve on a bed of rice and with a crisp salad.

Oranges in Tangerine Sauce

Serves 6   Preparation time: 30 minutes   Chilling time: Overnight

This dish can be prepared 2 days in advance if kept covered in the refrigerator.

6 seedless oranges, peeled, with
white pith removed

For the sauce:
225ml/8fl oz fresh tangerine juice
3 tablespoons sugar
1 teaspoon grenadine syrup
(optional)
1 teaspoon vanilla essence
3 tablespoons orange liqueur
Orange twists to garnish

---

1   For the sauce, place the tangerine juice, sugar, grenadine, if using, and vanilla in a saucepan and simmer until the mixture is reduced to 125ml/4fl oz.

---

2   Stir in the orange liqueur. Either slice or segment the oranges and place in a bowl. Pour the sauce over the orange, cover and chill overnight.

Serving suggestion: To serve, arrange the orange slices in individual goblets and spoon over the sauce. Serve garnished with twists of orange.

Orange Oatmeal Biscuits

Makes 24   Preparation time: 25 minutes   Cooking time: 15 minutes

100g/4oz plain flour
½ teaspoon bicarbonate of soda
½ teaspoon salt
100g/4oz butter or margarine
175g/6oz light brown sugar
1 egg
1 tablespoon grated orange rind
2 tablespoons fresh orange juice
75g/3oz oatmeal
75g/3oz raisins
50g/2oz chopped walnuts

Pre-heat the oven to 180°C/350°F/Gas Mark 4.

1   Lightly grease a baking tray. Sift together the flour, soda and salt and set
    aside. Using a blender or food processor, or by hand, beat together the butter,
    sugar and egg until fluffy. Beat in the orange rind and juice. Stir in the flour
    mixture, then stir in the oatmeal, raisins and nuts.

2   Drop tablespoons of the mixture on to the baking tray about 5cm/2in apart
    and bake for 15 minutes, or until golden. Cool on a wire rack before serving.

Serving suggestion: Ideal to serve as a teatime treat.

Oranges with Cointreau

Serves 6   Preparation time: 30 minutes   Chilling time: 5 hours

Here is a lovely refreshing dessert that can be served on its own, but is especially delicious served with vanilla ice-cream.

6 large, seedless oranges
175g/6oz sugar
150ml/¼ pint water
Juice of ½ lemon
2 tablespoons Cointreau

1   In order to peel the oranges easily, score the skin with a sharp knife, dividing each orange into quarters. Place the oranges into a large bowl, cover with boiling water and leave for 5 minutes.

2   Drain, and peel away the skin, gently scraping away any remaining white pith. Slice the oranges very thinly and place in a serving dish. Place the sugar and water in a saucepan and allow the sugar to dissolve over a low heat. Add the lemon juice and leave to stand for about 5 minutes. Add the Cointreau and pour over the fruit. Chill thoroughly in the refrigerator before serving.

Serving suggestion: Serve with fresh cream.

Duck à l'Orange

Serves 4   Preparation time: 1 hour   Cooking time: 2 hours

This recipe is extremely easy and quite delicious with all its varied flavours. It is best prepared the day before serving.

2kg/4½lb duck, cut into quarters
3 tablespoons oil
½ onion, thinly sliced
150g/5oz tinned tomatoes
2 bay-leaves
2 cloves garlic, thinly sliced
2.5cm/1in piece cinnamon stick
½ teaspoon dried thyme
2 whole cloves
Salt and freshly ground black
  pepper
225ml/8fl oz fresh orange juice
225ml/8fl oz chicken stock
Cooked rice to serve
Fresh parsley and orange slices
  to garnish

1   Pat the duck quarters dry with kitchen paper. In a large frying pan, heat the oil. Add the duck and onion and cook until brown on all sides.

2   Remove the breast pieces only and add to the pan the tomatoes, bay-leaves, garlic, cinnamon, thyme, cloves and seasoning. Stir over the heat for 5 minutes and then add the orange juice and stock. Bring to the boil, cover and simmer for 30 minutes, turning the duck every so often. Add the breast pieces, cover again and continue cooking until the duck is cooked and tender (1 hour). Turn the duck occasionally during cooking.

Serving suggestion: Before serving, remove the grease from the sauce. Remove the cinnamon, bay-leaves and cloves and adjust the seasoning. Serve the duck on a bed of rice with sauce spooned over and garnish with slices of orange and fresh parsley.

Note: If preparing this dish the day before serving, cool completely and store in the refrigerator overnight.

Lemon Chicken

Serves 4   Preparation time: see below   Cooking time: 40 minutes

This chicken recipe can be served hot or cold and is ideal to take on a picnic.

1.1kg/3lb chicken, cut into
  quarters
225ml/8fl oz fresh lemon juice
100g/4oz flour
1 teaspoon salt
1 teaspoon paprika
1 teaspoon freshly ground black
  pepper
50ml/2fl oz corn oil
1 tablespoon grated lemon rind
1 tablespoon brown sugar
50ml/2fl oz chicken stock
1 teaspoon lemon essence
1 lemon, thinly sliced

1   In a bowl, combine the chicken pieces and fresh lemon juice, cover and allow
    to marinate in the refrigerator overnight.

Pre-heat the oven to 180°C/350°F/Gas Mark 4.

2   Drain the chicken and pat dry with kitchen paper. In a plastic bag mix together
    the flour, salt, paprika and pepper. Shake well. Put one chicken piece into
    the bag at a time and shake until thoroughly covered.

3   In a frying pan, heat the corn oil and fry each coated chicken piece until
    brown and crisp (10 minutes). Transfer to a roasting pan and sprinkle with
    the lemon rind and brown sugar. Mix together the chicken stock and lemon
    essence and pour over and around the chicken. Place a lemon slice on each
    chicken piece and bake for 35—40 minutes or until the chicken is tender.

Serving suggestion: Lemon chicken can be served in many ways — with rice,
with cooked vegetables or with a light salad — perfect for all occasions.

Tuna Pâté-stuffed Lemons

Serves 4   Preparation time: 20 minutes

225g/8oz tinned tuna in oil
100g/4oz cream cheese
100g/4oz butter
Juice of ½ lemon
Salt and freshly ground black
  pepper
4 lemons
Fresh parsley to decorate

1 In a blender or food processor, blend together the tuna and oil, cream cheese, butter, lemon juice and seasoning to taste. Blend until completely smooth.

2 Take each lemon, cut the top off as a lid and level the bottom so that it will stand upright. Carefully remove all the pulp, keeping the skin intact. Fill each cavity with the tuna pâté, and decorate with fresh parsley.

Serving suggestion: Serve with hot, buttered toast.

Greek Lemon Soup

Serves 4   Preparation time: 15 minutes   Cooking time: 15 minutes

This rather unusual soup is refreshing and wholesome at any time of the day.

850ml/1½ pints chicken stock,
  strained with all fat removed
6 tablespoons rice
Salt to taste
2 eggs
Juice of 1 lemon

1 In a saucepan bring the stock to the boil and add the rice. Cook, covered,
   until the rice is tender. Season with salt to taste.

2 In a bowl, beat together the eggs and the lemon juice. Add to the bowl about
   100ml/4fl oz of the hot stock, stirring constantly. Pour back into the saucepan
   and heat over a low heat, stirring constantly. Do not allow to boil.

Serving suggestion: Serve immediately with fresh crusty rolls.

St Clement's Chequer-board Cake

Serves 6—8   Preparation time: 40 minutes   Cooking time: 25—30 minutes

Look at everyone's face when you cut into this cake — then see if they can guess how you made it.

For the sponge:
175g/6oz butter or margarine
175g/6oz sugar
3 eggs
225g/8oz self-raising flour, sifted
Pinch of salt
2 tablespoons milk
Grated rind of 1 orange and 1
  lemon
1 jar lemon curd

For the icing:
175g/6oz sifted icing sugar
50g/2oz unsalted butter
Finely-grated rind and juice of 1
  orange
Orange food colouring (optional)
Candied lemon and orange
  slices to garnish

Pre-heat the oven to 180°C/350°F/Gas Mark 4.
Microwave: Reduce the flour to 175g/6oz and make the cake batter as directed. Prepare the cake as below and cook on high power for 7 minutes. Leave to stand before turning out on to a wire rack to cool. Continue as directed.

1   Cream together the butter and sugar until light and fluffy. Beat in one egg at a time until thoroughly mixed. Fold in the flour with the salt and the milk. Divide the mixture between 2 bowls. To one add the grated lemon rind, to the other add the grated orange rind.

2　To prepare the tins, grease and flour 2 × 20cm/8in sandwich tins. Take 2 strips of foil 5cm/2in wide and fold each into a circle 15cm/6in across. Place in the centre of each tin. In one middle circle put half the lemon mixture and in the other tin put the remaining half of the lemon mixture into the outer circle. Do the exact reverse with the orange mixture. Carefully pull out the foil circles. Bake for 25—30 minutes until risen and slightly shrunk away from the sides of the tins. Remove from the tins and allow to cool on a wire rack. When cool, sandwich the 2 layers together with the lemon curd.

3　To make the icing, cream together the icing sugar and butter with the orange rind and juice and colouring if using. Cover the cake with the icing and decorate with the candied lemon and orange slice.

Serving suggestion: Serve on its own for maximum impact!

Heavenly Lemon Meringue

Serves 6—8   Preparation time: 1½ hours   Chilling time: overnight

Here's a dreamy version of a traditional favourite.

1 quantity meringue (see page
* 58)*

For the lemon filling:
4 egg yolks
75g/3oz sugar
1 tablespoon grated lemon rind
50ml/2fl oz lemon juice
125ml/4fl oz double cream

For the decoration:
125ml/4fl oz double cream,
* whipped*
2 tablespoons icing sugar

Pre-heat the oven to 140°C/275°F/Gas Mark 1.

---

1   First make the meringue as instructed.

---

2   Lightly grease a 23cm/9in pie dish. Spread two-thirds of the meringue into
    the bottom and use the rest to cover the sides, forming a mound around the
    rim. Bake in the low oven for 1 hour and then allow to cool on a wire rack.

---

3   To make the filling, beat the egg yolks with the sugar in a bowl set over a
    saucepan of simmering water. Beat well until thick and light in colour. Stir
    in the lemon rind and juice and continue cooking, stirring continuously. Beat
    the cream until thick and gently fold into the cooled lemon mixture. Spoon
    into the meringue shell and spread evenly. Cover with foil and chill in the
    refrigerator overnight.

Serving suggestion: Just before serving, mix together the whipped cream and
icing sugar and swirl over the top of the pie.

Cold Lemon Soufflé

Serves 10—12   Preparation time: 45 minutes   Chilling time: 4—5 hours

This dessert is so light and airy it's perfect after a heavy or rich meal.

5 eggs, separated
285g/10½oz caster sugar
Grated rind and juice of 3
  lemons
2 × 11g/½oz sachets powdered
  gelatine
100ml/4fl oz cold water
350ml/12fl oz whipping cream
Whipped cream and shelled
  pistachio nuts to decorate

1   First prepare a 1.1 litre/2 pint soufflé dish. Take a strip of greaseproof paper
    or foil large enough to encircle the soufflé dish, allowing 5cm/2in overlap.
    Fold in half lengthways. Butter the inside of the soufflé dish and the top third
    of the paper and sprinkle with caster sugar. Tie the paper around the dish,
    the sugar side on the inside.

2   In a bowl, beat together the egg yolks and sugar. Add the grated lemon rind,
    beat thoroughly, then very slowly add the lemon juice. Continue beating until
    very thick. In a small saucepan, soak the gelatine in the cold water. When
    the gelatine has absorbed all the water, allow it to dissolve over a very low
    heat until the gelatine has become liquefied. Do not allow it to boil. Leave
    to cool. Whip the cream until just light and fold into the egg and lemon mix-
    ture. Stir in the cooled gelatine until the mixture begins to set. Whip the egg
    whites until stiff and fold into the souffle mixture.

3   Pour into the soufflé dish which has already been prepared and chill thoroughly
    in the refrigerator for at least 4 hours (5 is better).

Serving suggestion: Just before serving, remove the paper collar and decorate
with piped rosettes of cream and pistachio nuts.

Key Lime Pie

Serves 8   Preparation time: 25 minutes   Chilling time: 5 hours

This exceptional dessert is a traditional favourite from the Florida Keys in the USA.

1 quantity biscuit crust
  (see page 25)
4 egg yolks
397g/14oz tin sweetened,
  condensed milk
125ml/4fl oz fresh lime juice
Green food colouring (optional)
225ml/8fl oz whipping cream,
  whipped
Lime twists to decorate

1   First prepare the biscuit crust and use it to line a 23cm/9in pie dish.

2   In a bowl beat the egg yolks well. Add the milk and beat together lightly. Add the lime juice, beat until smooth and add a few drops of green food colouring, if using. Pour into the biscuit crust, place in the refrigerator and chill thoroughly.

Serving suggestion: Spread the top with whipped cream and decorate with twists of lime.

Grilled Grapefruit with Kirsch

Serves 8   Preparation time: 20 minutes   Cooking time: 20 minutes

You can use either pink or yellow grapefruit for this starter. Either way, it is best served bubbling from the grill.

4 grapefruit, halved
100g/4oz sugar
100ml/4fl oz kirsch
Maraschino cherries or mint
   sprigs to garnish

1   Remove the seeds from each grapefruit half and, using a sharp knife, cut around each segment to loosen. Sprinkle each half with a little sugar and a little kirsch.

2   Heat the grill and set grapefruit halves about 10cm/4in from the heat (you may need to do 2 at a time, or possibly 4, depending on the size of your grill). Grill each one for 5 minutes until bubbling and brown.

Serving suggestion: Serve garnished with maraschino cherries or fresh mint sprigs.

Grapefruit and Avocado Salad

Serves 4—6   Preparation time: 40 minutes   Chilling time: 5 hours

This is a very pretty salad arranged and presented on a large platter, but it is the tangy and spicy dressing that really sets it off. Make the dressing in advance so that it can marinate with the garlic before serving.

For the special dressing:
175ml/6fl oz olive oil
50ml/2fl oz cider vinegar
Salt and freshly ground pepper
Dash of paprika
1 teaspoon sugar
1 teaspoon tomato ketchup
¼ teaspoon mustard
2 teaspoons lemon juice
½ teaspoon Worcestershire sauce
Dash tabasco
Dash celery salt
½ teaspoon horseradish
1 teaspoon chilli sauce
1 clove garlic, peeled

For the salad:
*1 iceberg lettuce, washed and
    trimmed*
*1 small cos, washed and
    trimmed*
*1 avocado, peeled, stoned and
    halved*
*1 large pink grapefruit, peeled
    and segmented*
50g/2oz celery, thinly sliced
*1 tablespoon freshly chopped
    chives*
Sprigs watercress to garnish

1   To make the salad dressing, combine all the ingredients except the garlic clove and beat well until blended and smooth. Place in a jar with the garlic clove and secure with a tight-fitting lid. Refrigerate for 5 hours. Remove the garlic and shake well just before serving.

2   For the salad, discard any bad leaves from the two lettuces. Wash, shake off any excess water, and place in the refrigerator to become crisp. Place the avocado and grapefruit in a bowl, spooning over any grapefruit juice to prevent discoloration. Cover and refrigerate.

Serving suggestion: Serve by arranging the greens on a serving platter. Slice each avocado half into 8 and arrange around the platter. Arrange the grapefruit segments in the centre. Sprinkle the celery and chives over the top and garnish with watercress. Serve the salad with the special salad dressing separately.

Glossary

Arrowroot A vegetable starch.

Bain-marie A double boiler. The French term for a large pot of hot water in which a smaller pot is placed to avoid direct heat.

Baking Blind To bake pastry cases prior to filling.

Baste To moisten a roast whilst cooking, using melted butter, gravy, stock, etc.

Beat To introduce air by way of beating or whisking to make light and fluffy.

Blanch To plunge fruits briefly into boiling water.

Candied Fruits coated with sugar, or turned partly or wholly to sugar.

Caramelise To melt sugar until just browned and liquefied.

Cassis Blackcurrant cordial.

Charlotte Pudding of fruit mixed with breadcrumbs and baked.

Chill To bring down to a temperature just above freezing.

Compote A mixture of fresh or dried fruits in a syrup, served as a dessert.

Croûtons Crisp pieces of toast or fried bread served with soups.

Custard A milk thickened with eggs or cornflour, brought to the boil over a bain-marie until thick.

Dredge To sprinkle evenly over the surface with flour, sugar or any other powder or fine granules.

Drizzle To sprinkle the surface with liquid.

Flambé To douse a cooked dish with spirits (brandy, for example) and set it alight.

Freeze To solidify food for storage by lowering the temperature to below 0°C/32°F.

Gelatine A brownish jelly-like substance obtained by boiling bones in water, which, on cooling, sets to a solid gel. Used in cooking, it acts as a stabiliser and aids the setting qualities of the dish.

Glaze To impart a shiny surface using eggs, gelatine, sugar, etc.

Hull To remove stalks of fruit.

Julienne Thin strips of meat, vegetables, etc.

Kirsch Cherry liqueur.

Knead The working of a dough by vigorous manipulation which strengthens the structure for the final baking.

Marinade Liquid used in marinating.

Marinate To steep meat, fish, etc., in a liquid in order to impart the liquid's flavours.

Meringue Baked mixture consisting of sugar and egg whites.

Pastry A stiff paste made with flour, fat, water or milk as a base for many confections.

Pâté Any paste made from meats, fish, etc.

Pie A pastry case containing sweet or savoury fillings.

Pith Inner skins — usually white and spongy — of citrus fruits.

Poach To cook in boiling water until soft.

Purée A smooth, sieved pulp.

Rind Tough outer skin of citrus fruits, etc.

Savory Aromatic herb.

Simmer To bring to just below boiling point.

Stock Liquid in which bones or vegetables are stewed. Used in soups, sauces, etc.

Syrup Natural juices of fruits; can also mean a sugar and water mixture used for glazing.

Soufflé A light dish made with beaten egg whites.

Springform Tin Baking tin with removable base.

Wheatmeal Flour which is milled to produce 85—90 per cent of the grain.

Whip To incorporate air into a mixture by beating the ingredients until light.

Whisk To use a wire whisk, to beat ingredients to a light sponge.

Wholemeal Flour made with 100 per cent of the grain ground either by roller mills or stones.

Zest The layer of the outer skin of citrus fruits used for flavour and garnish.

Index